From International Wrestler to Pubs and Punters

by
Johnny Kincaid

authorHOUSE®

AuthorHouse™ UK Ltd.
500 Avebury Boulevard
Central Milton Keynes, MK9 2BE
www.authorhouse.co.uk
Phone: 08001974150

© 2009 Johnny Kincaid. All rights reserved.

No part of this book may be reproduced, stored in a retrieval system, or transmitted by any means without the written permission of the author.

First published by AuthorHouse 12/22/2009

ISBN: 978-1-4343-0385-1 (sc)

This book is printed on acid-free paper.

ACKNOWLEDGEMENT

First and foremost I would like to thank my partner Hazel for putting up with my swearing and tantrums whilst writing this book, bless her for having the patience of a Saint.

Also I would like to thank Billy White Cloud for his friendship and sharing one of the most memorable wrestling trips that I ever made, and to all my wrestling colleagues that made me look good over the years.

To Danny and Gill, the best Pub management trainers ever, with out them I don't think I would have ever made it in the pub trade, hard work common sense and the occasional right hander prevails is what he said, and it was true, and that would be the same advice I would give to anyone wanting to take a pub now.

To Sasha and Ross and all the team at Authorhouse without them you would not be reading this book, a big hearty thanks.

And to all the unsuspecting people who without them there would be no book, their antics in the pubs I've had, good and bad, have left me with ever lasting memories; I thank every one of them.

And last but not least my very good friend Phil Treacy (known as Treacle to his friends) for helping me out over the years and for generally being there for me, thanks mate, and thanks for the kind words.

CONTENTS

ACKNOWLEDGEMENT	V
FOREWORD	IX
THE RED INDIAN BILLY WHITE CLOUD.	1
THE EMIRATES & BEIRUT	10
KOREA AND HAWAII	29
TRAINING AT THE LONGSHIP	60
THE BISCUIT MILL	73
THE BOW BELL	75
THE BLETCHLEY ARM'S	96
THE FIRST TRIP TO HAMBURG	104
THE BAD TIMES	107
PAULA, FIT FINLAY, AND THE BOY'S	121
THE KINCAID'S	123
BOMBER PAT ROACH	127
CELEBRITES	133
MY DOGS	146
THE BRADWELL MONK	155
THE WHITE HART	171

THE COURT CASE	**182**
THE ROYAL OAK	**184**
THE CAVENDISH ARMS	**198**
MY HIP REPLACEMENT	**203**
THE LONDON PRIDE	**219**
ABOUT THE AUTHOR	**239**

FOREWORD

When Johnny asked me to write this forward for his book I began to panic, what can I say about Johnny Kincaid? Something he cannot sue me over!! Well here goes. I first met John when I was invited to do a "stint" as a Disc Jockey at his pub in Bletchley, named after him, "Kincaids". This was the place to be on a Thursday, Friday and Saturday nights. The place was packed with people, shoulder to shoulder enjoying the music.

Many nights ended with us enjoying a drink, playing pool and putting the world to rights. This is also where I got to meet some of Johnny's wrestling friends and other stars from the world of entertainment. Memories of Ian Gillan (Lead Singer Of Deep Purple) running around the pool table naked with a rolled up page from a newspaper, alight tucked firmly into his buttocks.

When John moved to the Bradwell Monk pub, Wednesday nights became boy's night, during this time I owned a record shop and on Wednesday nights John would pick an album from the top 20 that he liked and we would play pool for it, and he would put up a pool trophy. He must have the best music collection in the world as he used to beat me every week, I did manage to win on one occasion!! and I treasure my trophy to this day, I'm convinced he let me win, but I would never tell him that.

Our friendship continued to grow over the years, so much so that I came to look on John as the big brother I never had, he became "Uncle John" to my children and likewise I met and integrated with his children.

My adventures with John over the years are too numerous to mention here, I could write my own book.

He is my friend, my confidant, my male soul mate, my best man but most of all, my brother. I will leave you with the words of a great man, a man that John has been likened to on many occasions.

"Friendship is the hardest thing in the world to explain. It's not something you learn in school. But if you haven't learned the meaning of friendship, you really haven't learned anything." All men have one refuge, a good friend, with whom you can weep and know that he does not smile.

-Muhammad Ali

THE RED INDIAN BILLY WHITE CLOUD.

I was sitting in the dressing room at the Guildhall Southampton when Billy White Cloud the Red Indian wrestler came to me and asked if he could stay over night at my house as he was leaving for Switzerland in the morning, I said 'I don't think there will be a problem with that, but I will have to phone my other half to see if she has made any other arrangements.' Billy had been over here in England for nearly a year. I first met him in Germany in the Hamburg Tournament, he looked good, he kept himself fit, he trained every day, he wasn't a big man as in tall, but he had a good physique, and for an American he had a good number of holds and counter holds which surprised most of us Brits that were in the tournament, as the American wrestlers are not known for there scientific wrestling skills, more for there crash bang wallop style, so it was refreshing to find one that could actually wrestle,

Before I left the tournament Billy asked if it would be possible to wrestle in England, I said if he gave me a photo of himself with all his particulars on the back like height, weight, and phone number, I would give it to my promoter and he would be in touch with him one way or the other. I had to leave the tournament a week before it finished, as I was due in Dubai a day after the end of the tournament, and I had promised the family that I would have at least a week at home before I went away again.

I sent Billy's photo's up to my promoter Brian Dixon, who lived in Birkenhead Liverpool, with a little message, looks good and can bloody wrestle, worth a try.

After spending three weeks in the United Arab Emirates I returned to have my first fight back in of all places Norwich in Norfolk England, the only nice thing about Norwich is the bloody roads leading out of it. I must say I had the surprise of my life when I entered the dressing room because who was sitting there was Billy White Cloud, "Buddy I owe you one" he said as he got to his feet and came over and shook my hand, from that day on we became instant friends. I made the phone call and as I thought there was no problem with Billy staying over, She said she would make up the bed in the spare room and there was also a message for me from a Mr David Hankestone the man from the Brewery,

I was playing with the Idea of going into the pub game after my wrestling career had finished, and wanted to find out more about it, but I never expected them to get back to me this fast, a week hadn't past since I sent the letter.

Billy and I stopped in a pub on the way home for a couple of beers, Billy was off to Switzerland the following day for a couple of fights then he was flying back to California, he said he didn't know if he would be coming back so we had to make the most of the time we had together, to be honest I really shouldn't have been driving that night because I had one or two too many.

The following day I took Billy to the airport, we said our good byes and he was gone, but something inside of me told me it wouldn't be the last time I would be seeing him. Later that day the Guy from the Brewery phoned again and we made arrangements to meet, the first words out of his mouth were, are you serious about taking a pub? 'I'm not crazy about writing letters, if I wasn't serious you would never had heard from me.' "Good" he said, "we have a pub for you now". 'Fucking hell' I said, 'that was quick'. "It's in Milton Keynes, go down on Friday and have a look and if you like it call me on Monday," 'OK, where is this Pub?' "On the Lakes Estate." Now I know the Lakes Estate, it was reputed to be the worst estate in Milton Keynes for violence. 'Are you sure you still have a pub there?' "Yes" he said, "we have just refurbished it". 'Why?' I asked, 'was it pulled apart?' "Have a talk to the governor his name is Ken, and if you like it call me on Monday, just keep an open mind" he said.

It was hard to keep an open mind when all the rumours you have heard about the Lakes Estate being the most violent Estate in and around Milton Keynes, you can't leave your car unattended when you go visiting, because you will have no wheels on it when you get back, that's if you have a car at all when you get back, and if you look at a person the wrong way they will smack you in the mouth then ask you who you were looking at,

I must be thick or crazy, because I said I would take a look on Friday Night and give him a call first thing Monday Morning.

It took the next two day to convince the other half there would be no harm in just looking at the place. When she saw the pub from the outside she said "that's it, lets go home", there was graffiti everywhere, some of it was quite artistic but most of it was really bad, not just the drawings but the language, who ever wrote the words couldn't spell. 'Now that were here,' I said lets just take a look in side; surely it couldn't be any worse. We entered through the side door, now this could have been my imagination, but you know when a cowboy enters a saloon and it all goes quite even the music stops, well that's how it seemed to me when Jean and I entered the Bow Bell, all eyes were on us. I either lost my hearing for the fifteen seconds it took to walk to the bar or nobody spoke, it seemed like I shouted for our drinks although I asked for them in a normal voice, then the sounds came back, people started talking again, to say it was a strange experience would be an understatement, 'Is the governor around'? I enquired of the bar maid, "he's upstairs she replied he'll be down in a while I suppose", 'thanks' I said. We stood at the bar supping our drinks and slowly looked around trying not to look too conspicuous, the place was a palace compared to the out side, new furniture, new carpet, even the back of the bar was new, there were steps leading up to an eye level, in all, this was a really nice bar, I was still looking around when this lady came up to me and said, "are you the new governors?" shocked, I replied 'I don't know, I'm just looking at the moment', she said "ho, well my names Phyllis and mine's half a Guinness. I laughed and said 'for your cheek I'll get you half a Guinness,' and she said, "I just asked what they were all thinking but too scared to ask, your a bit on the big side aren't ya". Just then the door behind the bar opened and a short stocky guy came through, I guessed this was the man I had come to see, the bar maid approached him and pointed to me, he came over still behind the bar and asked if he could help me, 'David Hankestone sent me down' I said, with that he flew from behind the bar as if he had wings on his feet, "what would you like to drink?" he asked. After we got our drinks we took a seat, he seemed to calm down, I sat there trying to work this guy out, he wasn't a tidy person his jacket was badly creased, his shirt collar was dirty and he had half his dinner down his tie, "my names Ken" he said, 'I'm John and this Is Jean'. Just then this woman joined us, "ho this is my wife Pauline", Ken said. "David Hankestone sent them down to look at the place," the look that I got, I didn't think it was worth offering my hand, I could instantly read what was going through her mind, it was nothing new, I had seen that look many times before, just then one of his customers came over, he was very polite, he said "excuse me but aren't you a wrestler, John, Johnny something? 'Kincaid' I replied, "that's right, Johnny Kincaid, you were on television a couple of weeks ago", Pauline's face lit up, "you A professional wrestler, well I never, and you want to take over MY pub". I thought to myself you two faced cow, a moment ago you were thinking, no not a black man taking over the pub, but now that a so called celebrity is interested in it, the black bit don't matter anymore, I never did like that woman, but Ken turned out to be a very nice and helpful guy.

Over the weekend Jean and I had many discussions about the Pub, the good points and the bad points. On the Friday night we were there the bar got quite full and the atmosphere was nice and jovial, there were a few loud characters but that makes for a good lively pub. It seemed that the bar was split into two sections, it was only one long bar but looking at the bar, to the right, which we will call the pool end was mostly occupied by Scotsman, and to the left of the bar was occupied by Londoners, they all seemed to mix very well, there was light banter going on but nobody took much notice of it, all in all the atmosphere was great.

Monday morning I made the phone call to Mr Hankestone, and told him I was pleasantly surprised with the pub, although it looked like a shit-hole from the outside.

"Graffiti can be removed" he said, "the question is are you interested? 'Yes' I replied, 'we are,' "good" he said, "I will arrange a formal interview and get the ball rolling, in the mean time if there is anything you want to know don't be afraid to ask Ken, he is a very helpful fellow". Believe me there were a lot of things I wanted to ask Ken.

I had only been behind a bar once or twice before, I had a friend (in Deanshanger a small village in Milton Keynes) who ran a pub, Jim and Sheila, it was Jim who suggested I should take a pub when my wrestling career finished, Jim had shown me a few things like changing a barrel and cleaning the lines, but I was sure there was a lot more to it, and there was, I kid you not. For the next week or two, every spare moment I got I was down the Bow Bell, and Ken was teaching me one thing or another on how to run a successful pub.

On the morning of our Interview for the pub I must admit I was shitting myself. Jean seemed to be taking it in her stride, cool calm and collected, me I was a bundle of nerves. I had wrestled in front of millions of people all over the world, but the thought of sitting in front of a hand full of people and answering questions scared the life out of me, I kept telling myself that I could answer any question that they threw at me, they couldn't ask me any questions about the pub game because I've never had one, so they could only ask personal questions, I think I was trying to convince myself that this interview was going to be easy, well it worked, when I walked into the office I was cool and calm, we sat there as if we had been interviewed a thousand times, and was used to it. Well Mr Kincaid one of the faces said, why do you want to leave your wrestling business and come into the pub game? 'I don't I said, what I mean is I don't want to leave the wrestling business and yes I still want to run a pub.' "But a pub will take up all your time," the face said. 'At first I'm sure it will but as time goes on I'm sure it will get easier, and I know a good few wrestlers that are running successful pub's and continuing their career as wrestlers, and one such person works for this company, Mr Steve Veidor.' All the faces looked at each other and

Johnny Kincaid

the main man said with a smile on his face, " you have answered all our questions in one tiny speech, thank you and we will be in touch."

On leaving the office Mr Hankestone was waiting for us. "How did it go Johnny?" he asked". 'I think it went all right I said'. " I will get you on a training course as soon as possible and get you into the pub." 'I'm sorry to disappoint you I said but I have a few contracts I have to finish first, so you are looking at least another four months before I am free to take on any kind of commitment to the Brewery.' "So be it" he said, "we will be in touch then". With a shake of Jean's hand then mine he was gone. "Hadn't you better tell him about your convictions? Jean said. She was right of course, I should have told him because if there's one thing that could stop me getting a pub licence is my police record of violence. Don't get me wrong, I'm not a violent person, and I have never hurt anybody who hasn't tried to hurt me first, but because of who I am and what I did for a living I was on a loser, it didn't matter that I was attacked first, it only mattered that my attacker got injured, so I end up with a police record of A.B.H or G.B.H. (Actual bodily harm, or Grievous bodily harm,) something is definitely not right with the justice system in this country, it was about a week after our interview when I got the phone call, the time was about four in the morning, I had not long been in bed as I had just driven back from Hamilton in Scotland. 'Hello' I said, "hi John" the voice said, I thought who the fucks calling me this time of the morning, "it's Billy" the voice said, 'Billy who' I asked, "Billy White Cloud" the voice said,

'Billy, do you know what the fucking time is mate' "holy shit, I've had a drink and I forgot the time difference" he said, (well we all know what the red Indians are like on fire water), 'what do you want Billy' I asked, "how would you like to come to Korea and Hawaii?" he asked. Now at this point you would have thought I would have be ecstatic, but I just told him to book me and phone me back, then I put the phone down and went back to sleep,

I said to the wife in the morning, 'I had a funny old dream last night, I dreamed that Billy White Cloud phoned me to go to Korea.' She said that she thought she heard the phone but wasn't sure, so no more was said, three days later Billy phoned back and said it was all booked, I would be flying out to Korea the following Month for three weeks then in to Hawaii for Peter Maivia for one week. 'Hold on a minute Billy' I said, 'what about the money side of things?' "Don't worry Johnny I have fixed it all up" and when he told me what I was getting, well lets put it this way, it's better he was on the other end of the phone, because if he was standing next to me he would have got a big kiss.

THE EMIRATES & BEIRUT

About two weeks following my interview with the brewery guy's I flew out to the united Arab Emirates for a two week tournament, first in Sharjah, then to Doha, then on to Bahrain. When we first arrived in Sharjah there was this guy waiting for Danny Lynch at the hotel, Danny had befriended him on his last trip there, and all he wanted to do was take Danny around to all his friends, Danny didn't mind because most of his friends were shop keepers and Danny was getting all sorts of things given him, like silk shirts hand made, safari suits made to measure, shoes made to measure, Danny loved it then who wouldn't. I shared a room with Danny on this trip, and this particular night we stayed out late and had a few drinks, the next morning somewhere around nine o'clock the phone rang, Danny shouted across from his bed "if its that fat little bastard tell him to fuck off, I answered the phone, 'hello I said,' "Mr Lunch the voice asked" (for some reason they couldn't say Lynch) 'no I replied Mr Lynch is still a sleep,' "but there is a man down here who wants to speak to Mr Lunch, he has a present for him," with hand over the mouth piece I said 'there's a guy down stairs who want s to speak to you, apparently he has a present for you,' "tell him to fuck off and come back later," 'Mr Lynch is very tired please tell him to call back later thank you' and with that I put the phone down. 'Listen you fat twat I'm not your fucking receptionist next time tell him your fucking self.' We climbed from our pits about eleven thirty, had a shower then went down for some breakfast, we were half way though our breakfast when I caught sight of the little fat man heading our way.

"Mr Lunch Mr Lunch" he was calling, Danny's face was getting redder and redder, I thought any minute now he's going to bust a blood vessel, when he reached our table Danny grabbed him and said "listen hear you little prick, its bad enough you calling my room at a silly hour, but don't ever interrupted me when I'm eating", "but Mr Lunch I never called your room this is the first time I come here to day and I beg your forgiveness for interrupting your food". Danny accepted his apologies and told him to wait in the reception area for him like a good boy. When we finished our breakfast we went to the reception desk, because Danny wanted to find out what prick had phoned our room this morning, the desk clerk said, "it was a messenger from some kind of sheik with a present for him", "a present said Danny what kind of present? He asked", "a Lincoln continental he said". "Did he leave it Danny asked?. "No the clerk said, he took it away again" Danny looked as sick as a pig on heat who couldn't get it up, 'never mind Danny its early, maybe he'll bring it back later.' It never happened, but Danny eventually laughed it off saying "the Sheik must have got a shock when the messenger returned with the car, and said Mr Lunch didn't want it, he wouldn't get out of bed for it". I remember one fight I had in Sharjah against an Indian wrestler called Ali Shan, he wasn't a very good wrestler but the arena was full of Indians and every time he managed to throw me they screamed like he was a world champion, he managed to throw me out of the ring once, you would have thought he had just been crowned president of the fucking world, I went to pick up a chair to climb back in the ring,

when this little Arab person grabbed it from me, I snatched it back and he went to make another grab for it, I lifted it above my head and the little bastard whipped me,

Yeh! I mean whipped me, you know the headgear that the Arabs wear, the sheet with the black cord that holds it on, well on this occasion it was thin shreds of bamboo and it fucking hurt, I said, 'you want the fucking chair that much, keep it,' as I threw the chair down the little guy went into a kung-fu stance, I thought to myself this guy has got to be joking, I jumped up onto the ring apron and as I stepped back into the ring I turned to see the little fella bow to me, I stood a good foot taller than him but he was willing to have a go, I thought he was either very stupid or he knew something that I didn't, personally, I think I could have got more heat from the little fella than I did from Ali Shan, and because the little guy had wound me up Ali Shan never got another look in, he was suplexed, body slammed, double elbowed, hyped, I nicked everything, not that I'm proud of myself for doing that, because I worked for me not for the show, and I shouldn't have let the little fella wind me up.

After the show and back at the hotel there was food and drinks laid on because there was some big Sheik that was at the show who wanted to meet the wrestlers privately.

I was shocked to see the little fella there, he kept looking my way and eventually when we were formally introduced he turned out to be the chief of police.

He wagged his finger at me and said in perfect English "you are a good enough wrestler not to have to use a chair on your opponent" I laughed and said, 'I was only going to use it to get back in the ring, (it was a very high ring,) and was there any need to whip me,' "I thought you were going to try and use the chair on me, and when you threw it at my feet I thought you were challenging me" 'I have a feeling that might have been a very bad move on my part' I said, he laughed and shook my hand "I have a feeling we are going to be friends" he said with a smile on his face, and at the end of the evening he gave me his headgear.

Every trip I made back to Sharjah I made a point of visiting my new found friend, one never knew when one would need help in a strange Country, and what could be better than having the chief of police as a friend.

There's not much I can say about Doha except it was a shit hole, I remember coming out of the hotel one morning and watching a Rolls Royce and a Lincoln Continental having a burn-up down the main street, they went around the fountain at the end of the road and back again, if you or I had either of those two car's, we would treat them with respect.

And the rat's we're nearly as big as cat's, a few of the boys and myself were having a drink in the hotel room, when one of them said come and have a look at this lad's, we went over to the window to look out as a car turned the corner and the head lights had shone onto this black mass that was moving down the back ally, "bloody hell" I said, the last time I saw that many rats together was In that film Ben, I was glad that we only had three day there.

Our next stop was in Bahrain, what a beautiful place, the buildings, the layout, the people, the only thing that spoilt it was the foreign tourist's. The Killer and I were walking down by the harbour and in the distance we saw some kid's diving of the harbour wall so we strolled over to have a closer look, what we saw wasn't very nice,

These three American guys' were throwing coins in the water and these young lad's were diving in to retrieve the money. What's wrong with that you're thinking to yourselves, nothing, if you're as sick as those American guys, the water was fairly clear except for the thin film of oil from the boats, and the shit and wood that was floating around, 'Why don't you just give them the coins?' I asked "There's no fun in that" one said. I looked at the one that spoke and said, 'would you dive into that shit?' "Like hell I would" he said. 'Well if you throw another coin in that water, you will be. I had it in my mind if he said another word he was going straight in, because I was in no mood to argue, the coins they where holding in their hands they just slapped down on the wall and walked away. Please don't get the impression that I think I'm a hard man, I'm not, but I had big John Kowalski (known as the Killer) standing behind me, and he's big enough to impress anybody.

(Mind you, you don't always have to be big to impress somebody, take the time I went to the Lebanon, for the second time). You meet some strange people when you travel around this world, take Beirut for instance, the Promoter one day took me to meet this guy, and as we approached the door he said "Mr Johnny, he has seen you before, you see him" I had no Idea what he was on about, but as I put my hand to the door it opened, we proceeded to walk down the corridor and entered a large well decorated office, behind the desk sat a man who was immaculately dressed, he left his well upholstered leather chair and approached me with his hand out saying "welcome to my Country Mr Johnny" as if it was his Country, "please be seated". I slowly looked around the office and noticed the three T.V.'s on the back wall, this is how he saw us, he had cameras panning up and down the street, and one directed on his door, he said "have you had a chance to see much of my Country yet" he asked, 'not as yet?' I replied, I have been to busy looking around for a suitable hotel for the rest of the wrestlers, when they arrive tomorrow.' (At this point I had better explain that Beirut is split in two, one half is Muslim, and the other half is Christian, and they weren't getting along very well, in fact they were at war with each other, they were throwing mortar bombs at each other as if they were presents, now you can imagine

I didn't want an hotel anywhere near the city centre, so I found one up in the mountains, it had everything you could want, a swimming pool, a shopping area, and a view over the City, (but you can't please everybody.)

Gabbeish, that's my new found friends name, had settled back down in his leather chair with his feet up on his desk and we were in polite conversation about everything in general, when all of a sudden the promoter jumped from his chair ran around the desk shouting look Johnny look, as he opened Gabby's, (as he liked to be called) jacket, on doing so he exposed a butt of a hand pistol, very nice I said, then he lifted one leg of his trousers exposing a gun in a holster strapped to his leg, the look that Gabby gave him was of a father letting his son have a bit of fun, he then went to a cupboard and on opening it I sat back in my chair, in front of me were shotguns,

M16 rifles, and hand grenades, 'expecting trouble I asked? "I never have trouble," he said. 'I can understand that' I said. "These silly people who want to shoot each other can't do it without weapons, business is business you understand", he said. "Of course I do,' I said. Not that I wanted to be around when he conducted his, on the way back to his seat the promoter picked up a brief case, now if looks could kill he would have been dead before God knew about it. Gabby was off his chair double quick and snatched the brief case out of his hand, it was a wonder he never broke his fingers. "Nobody touch this, nobody", as he cooled down he said, "I will show Mr Johnny." He laid the brief case on the coffee table and opened it, I don't know what I expected to see but all there was were a load of metal pieces, it took Gabby less that thirty seconds to assemble a Thompson machine gun, as proud as punch he said, "only one in Beirut, I have it imported from Chicago." With that he gave it to me, "don't touch trigger, no safety catch," he said. He promptly ordered the promoter to go and get a camera because he wanted a photo of me, and like a good little boy he went to fetch one. While he was gone Gabby gave me a quick run down on the promoter, he also said while I am in Beirut if there is anything I need I must phone him, any problems I must phone him.

It wasn't until after the photo shoot and we had left the office that I asked Adnan Ali how important a man was Gabby, with a smile on his face, he said, "very important Mr Johnny, he is the number one Mafia man in Beirut." My balls tightened and I nearly shit myself. I had been sitting, having a cigar, drinking coffee with the biggest gangster in Beirut and I didn't know it, there again what does a gangster look like, to me he was just like any other person you would meet on the street, he wasn't a big impressive man like the killer John Kowalski.

Johnny Kincaid

Trying to look like a gangster, but its not working.

The next day the rest of the guys arrived from England and Greece. After I settled them all down in the hotel I called a meeting to explain the situation concerning the hotel, why I had picked this one so far up the mountain, they all seemed to agree that it was better up in the mountain were there was not much chance of getting hit with a mortar, but after a few days one or two of them started to complain, they were getting fed up of staying in the hotel. I telephoned Gabby to see if he could help. "Hello Johnny" he said, "you have a problem?" 'No,' I said, 'we need a car, some of the boys are complaining that they can't get out or go anywhere and there getting rather restless and frustrated.' "Ok, what time do you need this auto? "He asked. I gave him a time and he said he would have one there for me.

We were all enjoying ourselves around the swimming pool when the guy from reception shouted, "Mr Johnny your auto is here," I shouted to the other guys 'do any of you guy's want to go for a ride? One or two of them shouted back, "where?" 'I don't give a shit, it was you lot that wanted to get out of the fucking hotel for a while.' With that there was a mad exodus for the door, by the time I got to the hotel door they were all just standing there looking at the car, except for one who had got in next to the driver. The car wasn't what I would call a stretch limousine but a semi stretch, "who the fuck do you know?" said Y.F. 'A very nice man,' I said. With that the driver said, "I will take you into the hills and show you our men", 'like fuck you will,' I said, they're shooting each other up there, we will take our chances in town, and that's were we went, not one gun shot or one mortar did we hear whilst there, it may have been a religious day, who knows, we where just thankful it was nice and quite.

I asked the driver if he would drop me off at Gabby's office and pick me up about an hour later, he told me that Mr Gabbeish had already asked him to do that, "oh," I said 'that's alright then.' As I approached the door as before there was a click and the door opened, the walk along the corridor didn't seem so long this time and Gabby met me at the office doorway, "my friend Mr Johnny, welcome," he said. "I thought we would go for a drink whilst you are in town and I will show you around our City," "what a great Idea," I said, we turned and walked back down the corridor, as he opened the street door I came face to face with three very smart gentlemen, they turned and walked to the car that was parked directly out side the door, one of the guy's opened the back door and ushered me in, then Gabby got in, then he got in beside Gabby, the other two climbed in the front next to the driver, we drove for about ten minutes then pulled up outside a large open fronted bar, we got out of the car the reverse of getting in, the two in front first, then the one next to Gabby, then Gabby, then me. When we were in the bar and having our first drink I said to Gabby, I can understand and appreciate the security around you but it does nothing for my underpants when I'm sitting next to you, anyone would have thought I had just told the funniest joke ever, he throw his head back and laughed out loud, I thought he was never going to stop, and when he did, he said "thank you, I have not laughed like that for such a long time, but you have not to worry, nothing will happen to you." "That's easy for you to say," I said, 'but I've seen the film The God Father,' with that he started laughing again uncontrollably, the three men sitting at a table in the corner were looking our way, and you could tell by the look on there faces what they were thinking, and by looking at them started me laughing, by the time we had stopped laughing we had tears running down our faces,

"Mr Johnny, you are the best thing that has happened to me for a long time, I can see we will be friends for a long-long time." 'How long is a long time in your line of business?' I asked. I shouldn't have said that because he started to laugh again and when he slapped the table the three guys jumped up, he shot his hand out quick as if to say stop, and they sat down again, we finished our drinks and left, Gabby was still laughing when he spoke to one of his men, the car pulled up and I was directed to the front of the car, one of the other guy's got in the back first then Gabby then another. I was seated between the driver and the other guy, Gabby spoke first, "I think the seating arrangement is better for you, you only have one pair of underpants with you I think." He started his uncontrollable laugh again, I said, 'I was only joking when I said I could shit my pants sitting next to you' but I don't think he heard me because he laughed all the way to the restaurant. When we entered the restaurant Gabby said "I have arranged a dinner party tomorrow night here for you and all your colleagues." The restaurant itself was quite quaint and picturesque, we stayed for another drink and a light snack, Gabby said he would be bringing his future wife to the dinner and he wanted me to introduce them both to all the wrestlers, of course I said, "it would be my pleasure." We finished our drinks and departed. We dropped Gabby off at his office and the driver took me back to the hotel, the rest of the boys had not arrived back yet so I had the swimming pool to my self, an hour or two later whilst I was catching up on my sun-tan the doors to the pool area opened and in they came, they were telling me where they had been and what they had seen. You know John one of them said, if there wasn't so many derelict buildings and the one's that were still standing didn't have so many bullet holes in, this would be a beautiful place, only one person was more interested in where I had been, and what I had been doing, not because he was really interested, he was more curious and nosy.

After the show that night I called the guy's together and told them, as we are not working tomorrow night we have been invited out to dinner, the cars will pick us up around nine o'clock so I would appreciate it if everybody would be in reception area at a quarter two nine, who ever is not there when the cars arrive will be left behind, no exceptions, I had to say that because I had two prima donna's with me, one was Greek and the other was English and they thought everything spiralled around them, and if they thought we were going to wait for them to make an appearance they had better make other plans.

All the next day D.L was trying to get out of me where I had been, and who arranged the dinner party, and was he involved in the wrestling show's, I said 'Danny do you remember what happened in Greece? Because if you don't you have a short memory, your only on this trip because the promoter said you were a big draw here once, so just do your work and keep your nose out of everything else.' Some how I just knew he was going to fuck the night up. The car's arrived and everybody was on time, D.L jumped in the first car and made sure he took up all the seat next to the driver, fortunately there was plenty of room for everybody in the two cars, on arrival at the restaurant we was met by the promoter who foolishly said, "tonight there is a free bar", when everybody had got there drinks I asked them to take there seats as I would like to introduce them to their host's, slowly they all took there seat's, D.L had made himself head of the table, which in my mind was the height of ignorance, because anybody would have known that your host is the head of the table,

How we never came to blow's God knows, I asked him to move but Gabby came from no where and took hold of my arm, "it doesn't matter Mr Johnny" he said as he led me back to the bar, "have a drink and stay calm," he was smiling and a sense of relief came over me, just then this beautiful woman appeared in the doorway, "ah she has arrived" said Gabby, as she walked towards us, no it was more of a glide, no, it was if she was floating towards us, everything was so perfect about her, the chiffon dress she was wearing, her hair, her earrings, her shoes, her hands, her finger nails, her smell, god her smell, pull your self together Kincaid I thought other wise you're a dead man. "This is my fiancé Mr Johnny, we are getting married in three months time", I took her hand and kissed it, "congratulations" I said, 'you must be the luckiest man in Beirut to have the most beautiful lest girl in the land,' steady Kincaid don't go over the top I thought, other wise it wont be just the lump in your trousers that will give your thoughts away, I finished my drink and asked if they would like to meet the wrestlers, "yes please" Gabby said, he sounded just like a school boy who was about to meet his favourite football Idol, I started at the lower end of the table where the three Lebanese wrestler sat, then moved on to the Greek wrestlers, I left it to Nick the tongue to pronounce their names for me, one by one they stood to shake hands and as we got to Danny, he stood , raised his hands above his head and growled, well she just took off and ran straight out the door, Gabby just stood there looking at him, and asked "why did you make this?, you make her run out of the door, maybe a auto hit her, maybe she is dead, if she is dead, you are also dead my friend", with that Gabby turned and walked away

'You fucking Idiot' I said to Danny, 'you don't know who he is, my advise to you is to get out of here now.'

Full marks to Danny he stayed where he was, but I'll tell you now, he was shitting himself after I explained who he was.

Gabby returned to the restaurant about an hour later, as he entered the restaurant with the three guy's I met the previous day, I thought fuck me he is going to shoot him.

Danny was out of his chair and walking towards Gabby when all of a sudden these three guys surrounded him, I heard Danny say, "I'm sorry for frightening your girl friend like that, but it was only meant as a joke." Gabby just stood there for a while looking at Danny, maybe trying to work him out. I could tell that Danny was a little perturbed by the sweat appearing on his scarred forehead, "ok" said Gabby "but you must think before you make a foolish move like this again", he shook Danny's hand and walked him back to his seat. "I trust the food is good, yes?" he asked. We all said it was excellent, not that Danny had eaten a morsel since Gabby had gone, and I had told him who he was, he had done the right thing by staying, because there was no way he would have got out of Beirut if anything had happened to Gabby's girl.

The rest of the night went quite well with lots of laughter, and showing of hand pistols. (See photos).

**Gabbish pointing the gun at Danny's head, I was
just glad that he was in a good mood.**

The last day of the trip Gabby invited me to his house for a drink and asked me if I had any problems in England, 'how do you mean?' I asked. "The black and white situation" he said. He had been watching the news on T.V and the Brixton riots were being shown, 'I'm a sports-man and we don't encounter that kind of shit' I said, he smiled, and said "maybe one day you have a problem, you must remember to phone Gabbish, no more problem", on the way out Gabby gave me a present which I have treasured from that day to this.

Three Months later I received an invitation and an open airline ticket in the post to attend his wedding, but unfortunately I couldn't go as I was booked out in India at the same time, we stayed in touch for a number of years but then the letters stopped coming, I never could find out if anything had happened to my friend.

For those of you that don't know of Dangerous Danny Lynch, he stood Five foot seven inches, weighed in around twenty four stone, and had scars on his forehead that looked like Clapham junction railway lines, not a pretty sight.

I could never understand why British wrestlers always undervalued themselves and others when they went abroad. I remember flying out to Nigeria with one of our top M.C's Mr John Harris, when we were at Heathrow airport I noticed two other big guy's from the American wrestling scene, Dusty Rhodes and Hangman Bobby Jagars, I was wondering where they were going, they got on the same plane as us for the short trip to France. When we took off from Charles-De Gaulle airport in France they could only be going to one place, Lagos in Nigeria, so I wandered up to where they were sitting and introduced myself, they seemed to be two nice guy's. When we arrived in Lagos the four of us were taken to a hotel, it wasn't a very nice hotel; in fact it was a shit-hole. I was sharing a room with John; our cases were open on the bed when we heard this commotion going on outside, it was Dusty and Bobby. "If you think we're staying in a shit hole like this you're very much mistaken" I heard Dusty say. 'Come on John grab your bag' I said 'we're moving hotels,'"we can't do that"

said John, 'what's good for them mate is good for me' I said, 'I'm off, are you coming?' John grabbed his bag, and our cab followed Dusty's to the Intercontinental

Hotel, and do you know, not a word was said by the promoter, funny that.

The American dream Dusty Rhodes trying to out pose me

I was the booker for wrestlers into Zambia for seven trips, and the wrestlers I took out there we're on top money, a lot more than the opposition promoter was paying, but one sneaky bastard undercut me and said he could get wrestlers cheaper than I could, you just cant help some people, so it's no wonder that a lot of the boy's just look after number one. If only we we're more like the American's, they don't take any bullshit.

The same thing happened to me in Greece, everything was going nicely, I had done about five trips with various wrestlers when one day the promoter asked me if I could bring a wrestling ring out with me the next time I came, I said "sorry I couldn't do that" the reason was I could never bring myself to fully trust a Greek promoter again, I was once knocked by a Greek promoter for all my wages, that's why I made sure all my guy's got their money each night before they wrestled, and if I had brought a ring out for him and anything went wrong I would have been in shit street trying to get it back out of Greece and driving it home.

Now having said all that, there was this particular wrestler who was listening to our conversation, and went behind my back, and told the promoter he could bring a ring out for him, and get wrestlers cheaper than I could, hence, Johnny was dropped again, the wrestler who shat on me got shat on himself, and as the old saying goes, if you pay peanuts you get monkeys, they were having some poor shows in and around Athens, all the wrestlers got knocked for their money when the promoter went missing, and on the way home the car broke down, to cut a long story short he lost everything, the car, the ring, the lot. What goes around comes around as they say. (After Bahrain I returned home)

KOREA AND HAWAII

It was a Thursday morning and I was leaving for Heathrow airport, I had already picked my tickets up from Pan-am offices in the west-end of London, I had checked my bags half a dozen times, you know what its like, you always think you have forgotten something, and nine times out of ten you have, (I forgot my wrestling boots on one trip) anyway, with everything packed, (I kissed the dog, and tapped the wife on the head, or was it the other way around?), and then I was on my way.

It was one hell of a long flight, first stop was in Anchorage Alaska where we stayed for an hour or so while the plane refuelled, the flight to Anchorage was nice and smooth but the sight of all those icebergs beneath us was just awesome, it was about four hours after take off that I arrived in Hawaii (Honolulu), it was like I had been dropped in the middle of one of Elvis Presley's film set's, on departing from the plane and the heat hitting me and entering the terminal to the cool air-conditioning, and then having a gorgeous girl put a flowery garland around your neck, I was in love, I thought this must be what heaven is like, everything seemed so perfect.

So far so good everything was going to plan, I made my way through to customs, on handing my passport over I kept my fingers crossed hoping my visa and everything else was in order, it was, thank God, I collected my bag's from the carousel, now all I had to do was find the person who was to meet me in arrivals. As I stepped though into the main hall carrying my bags this sweet young thing said "Mr Kincaid," I looked, she said again "Mr Johnny Kincaid," with a nod of my head I said 'yes,' "I have come to take you to your hotel, you will be staying one night, then tomorrow I will pick you up and bring you back to the airport at three thirty p.m, you will catch your flight to Soul in Korea at five p.m," just as I was thinking does this girl ever stop for breath we arrived at the car-port where this young guy took my bags and threw them in the boot of the Cadillac, (I've seen them in films but I had never ridden in one, there so spacious and comfortable), the young guy was the boy friend of the sweet young thing, well I didn't mind really because at this time I was more interested in the bloody car, he opened the back door for me to get in but I ushered the young lady in and said 'I would like to ride up front with you if you don't mind,' he didn't, and the journey too the hotel was not only filled with beautiful sights but it was very informative as well, my hotel was just off the strip of Waikiki and my hotel room faced the Diamond Head, that's a fucking big rock looking out over the sea, apparently if you see it from the air it looks like a bloody great diamond, hence the name Diamond Head. On arrival at the hotel my young friend booked me in, then asked if I would like to eat with them later after I'd had a little rest, 'that would be very nice' I said and made arrangements to meet up with them around eight thirty, the time was around two in the afternoon and I was feeling bloody shattered, the jet lag was catching up with me, Honolulu is ten hours behind England so therefore it would be midnight at home, was it a wonder I was fucking knackered and wanted my bed, I asked the guy in reception if he would give me a call about seven o'clock, because I had the feeling that the alarm on my watch was never going to wake me up, and I was right. At five past seven I was woken with a faint ringing in my ear, I lifted the phone and a voice said to me "Mr Kincaid you are alive? I have been ringing your room for the past five minutes", 'thank you for your patience's I really needed that sleep.' I was out of bed and in the shower in the next few minutes, I was feeling like a new man already and it was just sinking in where I was, when I saw a picture on the opposite wall of Waikiki Beach and the sun-set, what a beautiful sight.

At five past eight I took the lift down to the reception area were I was to meet my two new friends, as I was early I thought I would make for the bar and have a couple of lagers while I waited for them. I entered the bar which was situated at the back of the hotel, a cosy little place with a guy playing a piano, I remember as I walked to the bar there was this girl sitting at a table just in front of the bar and her eyes seemed to burn into me, well that's what I thought anyway, I ordered my drink and slowly turned around and there she was still looking my way, I was thinking to myself, play it cool Kincaid she could be a working girl, I took another couple of swigs of my lager and slowly turned around to find a guy sitting in the opposite seat to the girl, bollocks I thought, well it is only my first night what's my rush, by the time I had finished my first glass of lager my two new compadres had arrived, "hi Johnny are we ready to go?" the guy said, (for the life of me I can't remember their names) 'ever ready that's me' I said, they had a taxi waiting out side, we drove along Waikiki beach towards Diamond Head, "I have booked a table at the Black Pearl Restaurant on the other side of the Head, you will see the difference between this side and the other side, this is the relaxing and sunbathing side of the rock, the other side is for sport".

We took our seats in the Restaurant, which looked out of a large plate window over looking the Pacific Ocean, it was fantastic but for the life of me I will never understand why they call Surfing a sport, it's more like suicide. From where we sat in the Restaurant we could see for about a quarter of a mile along the beach and there were these suicide people paddling their boards out so far that they looked like dot's in the water, then in they came on this little wave that seemed to get bigger and bigger until it was (and I kid you not) at least twenty or twenty five feet high, are they fucking mad or what, my two friends were laughing at the way I was carrying on, the girl said, "this is our national sport, people come from all over the world to take part in the Surfing Championships, even people from England." I thought, mad dogs and Englishmen as they say, it could be right after all. While I was thinking, the guy said, "come Johnny it is nearly time." We left our seats and joined most of the other people from the Restaurant and went out side onto the veranda, the sight was magnificent, I can honestly say without sounding like a prick, that it's the best sight I'd ever seen, the sun seemed that big that you could reach out and touch it, I watched it slowly sink out of sight over the Ocean, to say I was moved would be an understatement, as was every other foreigner standing on that veranda, there was only one thing that could beat that, and I will come to that later.

The meal was fantastic, and the evening was rounded off with a cabaret of Hawaiian singer's and dancers, all in all it was a magical night.

The next day as promised they arrived at the hotel to take me back to the airport, we said our good bye's and I thanked them for their hospitality, and said I hoped to see them again in a few weeks, with that I was off to catch my plane to Korea.

As I came through the gate at Soul International Airport there was a friendly face there to greet me, beaming from head to foot stood Billy White Cloud in his buck skins, the only thing missing was his feathered head dress, "hi Johnny, did you have a good flight?" he asked. 'What can be good about sitting on your arse for six hours on a bumpy plane?' I said. 'To answer your question the answer is no, it was the fucking shits, I had never been over so many hump back bridges, and the food was cold, and there wasn't a decent looking girl on the flight and that's including the air hostesses.'

"Ok". Said Billy, "lets go and get some breakfast then I will take you to our hotel and fill you in what's happening out here", 'great' I said 'but what's this breakfast business it's only 11.25 at night by my watch,' "yes" he said "by your watch, but it's twenty past eight in the morning here, we're nine hours in front of Hawaii," 'fuck me I said I'm never going to catch up on my sleep at this rate.' I tried to stay awake as long as possible but around midday I couldn't keep my peepers open any longer, so I snatched a couple of hours sleep, I didn't want to sleep too long because I wanted to be tired around ten o'clock at night, so I could get a good nights sleep and get rid of the jet lag. It worked but the following day I felt like shit, the body ached, and if I had pulled a girl I couldn't have raised a good gallop, now that's bad, that's how drained I felt, in three days three different time zones, my body clock was completely fucked.

From International Wrestler to Pubs and Punters

CHIEF BILLY WHITECLOUD
RED INDIAN STAR – INTERNATIONAL WRESTLER

Billy became a life long friend.

Johnny Kincaid

Billy met me in the reception with a few of the other foreign wrestlers, a big guy from Malibu called Hippo, he weighed in about twenty two stone looked more like a Sumo wrestler, another guy from the states Bobby Heenan, a Japanese referee called Kiyomigawa and another guy from the states called Rocky Johnson, this fella had twenty one and a half inch biceps, now that's what I call big arms, he didn't have such a fantastic physique but his arms, fucking hell they were big, there was also a guy from Italy, Salvatore Bellomo, a very good looking Italian, I could see I was going to have competition, if you know what I mean.

We all hung around with each other for the rest of the day creating havoc wherever we went, in shop's in restaurants, people would come in just too look at us, they would follow us along the road, we even created a traffic jam on one of the main roads, we should have charged for the autographs we signed, we could have made a fortune, but to be honest we were all thankful when we arrived back to the air conditioning of the hotel, man it was hot out there. The first match I had out there was a tag-match with Billy as my partner, we were up against these two Koreans guy's that surprised Billy and I because they could wrestle, not very well but they had the basics, and they weren't dangerous and that was the main thing. Billy and I could work with them and we made a fairly good bout out of it, we made them look like superstars before we beat them, if we went straight in and beat them then what have we beaten? Nothing, but if we make them look like the best thing since slice bread then beat them, then we've beaten the best. After the match they both came to Billy and I very excited and bowing all the time, we couldn't understand a word they were saying, but I think they were trying to say thank you. It must have been the best bout they were ever involved in. Billy and me were just happy to come out of it without any injuries and winning our first match. Later that night in the restaurant the promoter came in with this giant of a man (who said that all Koreans were small?) who stood at least seven feet two inches, "this is the Champion of Korea" he said, I would never have guessed I thought to myself, it was hard trying to have a conversation with him, he never spoke a fucking word of English everything had to be translated, I made it easy for him by not trying to talk, just gesturing, like photo, and showing him the camera, he stood up to his full height and wanted me to stand by the side of him, what am I some kind of prick, this photo's for me not him to show how big and tall he is beside me, 'sit down you twat the photo will still show what a big ugly bastard you are' thank god he couldn't understand a word I was saying, one of his hands was the size of two of mine put together, and if he slapped me it would be goodbye from me forever, he turned out to be an alright kind of guy.

My second bout was against Bobby Heenan in a town called Songnam, a very colourful town a brightly lit place, it reminded me of the west end of London, neon lights and plenty of coloured bulbs, everyone we met seemed very friendly and happy to see us, we found some of the younger children could speak English but very few of the adults could or didn't want to, but they all had smiles on there faces, like Soul we wrestled in a very big leisure centre and it was full, this promoter must have done one hell of a job promoting his shows because it was at least fourteen years since they last had wrestling here, so far two shows and two full houses, my bout with Bobby was something else, a mixture of American style and English Technical style, it was fast and furious, him with his crash bang wallop style and me with my quick fancy moves, we did a twenty minute draw and I was puffing out of my arse at the end, it was non stop movement from start to finish, the only consolation was he was as fucked as me, all the boy's who had been watching the fight came to us and said that was some show, it was the first time Bobby and I had ever worked together and when your peers give you praise like that it means a lot, the punters also liked it because they were up and down in there seats like a fucking yoyo, thank god we had a few days off, it gave our body's time to recuperate.

The next stop was in a place called Wonju, again a fairly large town with plenty of bright lights, all the towns seem similar in that sense, our hotel was just off the main street so we didn't hear the rush of cars and scooters driving by all night, after booking into the hotel, Billy, Salvatore, and myself went for a walk around town, and what we noticed was, the girls here seemed more friendly, they smiled back at you instead of laughing and hiding there faces. We stopped at this café come bar place for a coffee, the girl that served us made eye contact with Salvatore, she wasn't the best looking Korean girl we had seen but once they make eye contact with him he is in there knickers, he wrote his name and hotel on a napkin with the message please phone, we all new she would, it was the way she looked at him every time she passed the table, the look of someone climaxing in there knickers, to cut a long story short, she phoned, they met, and she was a noisy fuck, how do I know this? because I was in the room next door and couldn't help but hear, one up to Salvo.

The audience at the auditoriums have so far mostly been male, but this night it was a good mixture of both sexes and the atmosphere was totally different, the people expressed them selves more freely, (let me explain) in Soul, Rocky Johnson was wrestling this Korean guy and giving him a good pasting, there was hardly any reaction from the male members of the audience, but here in Wonju the male members of the audience and some of the females were really getting involved in the action, was it because the males wanted to show off in front of their women and show they weren't scared of the wrestlers, who knows, but it created a great atmosphere to work too. I was matched with one of the Korean lads that I wrestled in the tag match on the first night, now' I was debating with myself whether to try and give this fella a clean technical bout, or go villain on him right from the start. I decided on the technical side and if I couldn't pull it off, I could always turn villain.

There were two young ladies that came in with one guy now unless they are meeting someone else there is one lady spare, I kept my eye on them to see where they were seated, second row, blue corner. I kept my eyes open just in case there were any loose women around, meaning girls by them selves or two girls together, Salvo was already one up on me.

My match was a twenty minute time limit but there was no way it was going to go that long, I chose the blue corner for obvious reasons. As I approached the ring the punters were holding out their hands to be touched, I think they had been watching the American wrestling on T.V because that's what all the yank wrestlers do, run around the ring touching hands then diving in the ring, well, I walked slowly around the ring with my usual smile on my face, touching hands, ruffling kids hair up, stopping to ask a punter if he's had a good day, not that he could understand a fucking word I was on about but as I was nodding my head so was he, I stopped to ask an old boy who was sitting directly in front of the guy and the two girls if he had had a good day as I looked up I noticed an old lady sitting next to one of the girls with the guy sitting next to the other, so I assumed the girl sitting next to him was his, so I did the famous double take, I looked at the other one, looked at the old fella, then straight back at her and held her glance just long enough for a big smile to come to my face, I shook the old mans hand turned and jumped up onto the ring, turned' and looked at her again, she was smiling back at me, the next move was to meet her but that would have to wait until after the match.

It would have been so easy to turn this guy into a villain, and he wouldn't even have noticed, it was a much slower fight than the one I had with Bobby, I had to be a bit cautious in case he got excited and carried away with himself, then he would become dangerous, I always want a good bout so I would always help the other guy provided they would let me help them, and this guy did, we had a cracker of a bout, it only lasted about twelve minute but in that twelve minutes he threw me from arsehole to breakfast time, he put me in holds he never new existed and he must have thought he was Houdini because he got out of holds he had never seen before, I never put myself in any position where he could possibly hurt me or pin me, so he had a good run then I pined him. The promoter was happy which made me happy, and the young lad was over the moon.

Now back to the serious business of pulling this girl. I spoke to our interpreter to see what he could come up with. "In the interval I will see what I can do for you but I can not promise anything you understand." 'I understand that' I said, we only have one more day in this town then we're off again so it's now or never. Later he came to me and said, "sorry Johnny, she is with her brother and sister-in-law and there is no way she can leave them, she said thank you for the interest but there is nothing she can do." Well isn't that polite I thought to myself, bollocks, fuck, shit, well I had to let off steam some how, Billy and I went to get a cola and was stopped by a few punters for autographs. We were signing them when the girl appeared in front of me with a piece of paper, here we go I thought, a message of some sort, like fuck, all she wanted was my autograph, I wanted to write bollocks on it but I didn't, I wrote with love, she smiled and said sorry in perfect English and then she was gone.

Suwon was about eighty miles from Wonju and we had three days there. The first day it rained cats and dogs all day and all night, the following day the sun came out and stayed out and it shined on me. I was taking a walk around town with Bobby, Rocky, and Salvo, we had just left an apartment store when we heard some one calling Johnny, as far as I knew there was only one Johnny there but we all turned to see who was calling me, there she was walking towards me with a big smile on her face, the girl from Wonju, 'what are you doing here?' I said 'I thought I would never see you again.' "I am visiting relatives, the man who spoke to me in Wonju said you were going to fight here so I thought it would be a good time to visit, I was going to come to the fights tomorrow to surprise you but you surprised me." The rest of the guys were just standing there with there mouths open, not only have I pulled, but she speaks bloody good English as well, she learnt her English at university in Soul where she studied medicine and now she worked as a pharmacist in Wonju. Needless to say I waved the boys good bye and we took off, she showed me around town then took me to meet her grand parents that looked about a hundred forty, but I learnt later that they were only in their sixty's (they must have had a hard life). We went out later to a restaurant I took the grand parents with us and believe it or not we all had a good time, we sat in that restaurant for about three hours taking our time and nobody rushed us to finish, it was amazing, try doing that in England, by the time we had finished it was quite late, she looked at me and

From International Wrestler to Pubs and Punters

asked if I wanted to stay over night, I looked at her and said 'I would love to stop with you all night, but at the hotel, not at your grand parents place, there's not much room there and the walls look very thin,' she put her hand to her mouth and started laughing, we got a cab back to the grand parents place and dropped them off, after saying my good bye's I looked at her and asked her 'what's happening now?' "we go to your hotel" she said, "but I must take something from the house first," she disappeared inside with her grand parents, I thought that would be the last I would see of her, but she reappeared a couple of minutes later with an over night bag, yipeeeeeeeeee.

She stood about five foot one inch and weighed roughly six and half, or maybe seven stone, she had black shoulder length hair; and was of slight build meaning she didn't have big tits but small firm ones, she wasn't beautiful but attractive, but she smelt divine. She went into the bathroom and spent at least fifteen to twenty minutes doing what? Fuck knows, then it was my turn, I had a piss, cleaned my teeth, washed my bits and pieces then I was out, all done in five minutes flat, she was already in bed when I returned, I slipped of my pants and got in beside her, she felt so small and fragile in my arms like a piece of porcelain, "Johnny" she said, "please don't hurt me, you are so big" now she wasn't talking about my lower bits, because who ever said that black men had big dicks were telling lies, ok, maybe they have, but I'm only half-cast and only got half share.

This was my first sexual encounter in nearly a week and I was going to make the most of it, and I did, she must have thought I was going through the karma-sutra but she never complained, half the time I let her take the initiative so she could do what she liked best, it's nice when a woman takes over, it turns a guy on so much knowing that she really wants your salami, it was about six o'clock in the morning when I awoke with this beautiful sensation going though my lower region, I opened my eyes and looked down, the sheet that was covering me was going up and down, as I pulled it off, her eyes were looking straight into mine whilst she kept the motion going, a little while later she slithered up my body and sat down on me, I could hardly feel her weight, she was like a feather, some time later she just collapsed on me, we were both sweating and panting like a couple of old sheep dogs.

It's like having sex for the very first time, you never forget, and you never forget your first sexual encounter in a strange country. I only had one more sexual encounter in Korea, but I remember Salvatore beating me by about three, the bastard.

Our last show was back in Soul, It was in a tag-match with Rocky Johnson as my partner, we were against Salvatore and Bobby, I watched the two Korean lads tear each other apart, I couldn't believe what I was watching, it didn't seem that they we're the same two lads that had given Billy and myself a half decent match, their whole professionalism had gone out of the window, they had no timing, nothing, when they came in the dressing room they were both bleeding from their nose, mouth, one had a bloody big scratch down his neck behind his ear, and the other had a small gash over his eye, the promoter went over to them put his arms around them and spoke in Korean, when he had finished he came to us and said with a big smile on his face, "I told one that he was better than the other and he should win, then I told the other one that he was better, and he could beat the other, then I told them both it would be good if there was some blood tonight". Little did he realize that he nearly had a fucking murder on his hands?

The following day we all had to meet at the immigration office for the taxes to be paid on our work permits, we all arrived about ten o'clock in the morning looking a bit worse for wear, we were sitting around for about an hour when our interpreter arrived looking very worried. "What's the problem? Rocky asked." "The Boss man should have been here yesterday to pay everything but he hasn't, and no one knows where he is now." 'Shit' I said, "that's bullshit" said everyone else, "so what happens now?" said Bobby. "We have to wait until he is found, they won't let us leave until the taxes have been paid and they have stamped our passports, to show that they have been paid at the customs." Now everybody is thinking the worst, that the dodgy bastard had done a runner with the money.

An hour or so later he walked through the doors of the immigration office as if nothing had happened, "Hi guys" he said, "sorry I'm late, I had business in Wonju but it took a little longer than expected," he could have been killed within an instant, but the relief of seeing him was quite evident by the look on everyone's face, the thought of being locked up was going through everyone's minds, so he was forgiven just as fast.

Now were smiling, we'er free men

At the airport we were all saying our good bye's, hugging and shaking hands as if we had known each other for years, saying we hope to meet up again sometime in the future knowing full well its highly unlikely, but stranger things have happened.

Kiyomigawa was off back to Japan, Bobby and Hippo were flying back to the States, and Salvatore was going to Germany for a tournament in Hannover, I asked him to relay my best wishes to some very good friends of mine who work quite regular in Hannover,

(Tony St Claire, Dave Fit Finnley, Mal Kojak Kirk, and the Giant Haystacks).

Rocky was coming with Billy and myself to Hawaii, our flight was at a quarter past eight at night, but on arrival in Honolulu it was only eleven o'clock in the morning of the same day, here we go again I thought, fucking about with my body clock again. I was sitting next to Rocky on the flight over and he was talking about seeing his son, he didn't like being away from him for to long. 'So your meeting your wife and kid in Honolulu then? I asked.' "We have a house there, as well as one in the States" he told me, 'It's all right for some, well I know where to come for a holiday' I said, "any time" was his answer. On arrival the sun was high in the sky, and everyone was smiling, I thought to myself, Johnny boy, you only have a week here son, make the most of it, so after getting through the formalities of the customs and picking up our bags, we made our way through to the customs area into the main hall where Rocky met his wife and child, he introduced Billy and myself to her and I must say she was quite a looker, then he said "and this is my son Dwayne", you could tell straight away that Rocky was so proud of him, the body language said it all, he couldn't keep his hands off him, picking him up, twisting him around, he had missed his son, Rocky then surprised me, "you'll be staying at the Korean Plaza, that's where dad puts all his foreign wrestlers, I'll phone you there in a couple of days then you and Billy can come around for dinner" he said, we shook hands then he was on his way with his son sitting on his shoulders, I looked at Billy and said 'did I hear right, did he call the promoter dad?.' "Yeh, Rocky's married to Peter Maivia's Daughter, she's a true Princess," well fuck me; you learn something new every day.

Bill and I made our way over to Hertz car rentals, as we were staying for a week we thought it would be better to hire a car than take public transport every where, at least that way we can travel all over the island and see the bits that the tourist don't normally see, it's more interesting that way.

We found our way to the hotel, it was two blocks back from Waikiki beach but nearer to the Head than the other hotel I stayed in, by the time we unpacked our cases the time was about two thirty in the afternoon but my body clock was telling me it was around eleven thirty at night, I said to Billy I think a few beers are in order then we will try and stay awake for as long as possible, he agreed, so we made our way to the nearest bar and sunk a few Bud's, quite a few Bud's, it was the best nights sleep I had had for a long time.

I awoke to the sound of some one tapping on my door and a voice saying room service, some ones having a fucking laugh I thought, I got out of bed and put on the dressing gown that was hanging on the back of the door, as I opened the door this guy with a trolley said "your breakfast Sir," 'I didn't order any breakfast' I said, "no but I did," Billy said as he put his head around the door, it's twenty past ten, are you getting up today?" After showering, I felt like a new man ready to face the world, "what's on the agenda for today? I asked Billy, as we stepped out of the hotel into the bright sunlight,

"Fancy a run down to Pearl-Harbour, we can spend the day down there looking around the ships, and then we can get a boat over to the S.S.Arizona monument" he said, I'm not much of a nautical man but when I saw the size of some of those ships I couldn't wait to get on them, I was like a kid all over again. During the day we had boarded battleships, destroyers, frigates, and aircraft-carriers, and even a submarine, ok it was a world war two job but that don't count, the last port of call was the monument in the middle of Pearl-Harbour which stood over the remains of the S.S.Arizona the first ship to go down with all its crew, it was a weird feeling standing there looking out at a gun turret just appearing above the water knowing that beneath you is the remains of all the crew that died on that ship, entombed there forever, when you have seen something like that you feel so insignificant, all those men that died in one spot wondering what the fuck was going on. I felt very humble as I stepped back on the boat to take us ashore; I also had a tear in my eye.

Later that evening Billy and I took a walk along the front of Waikiki beach there was still a lot of people around on the beach so we stayed on the roadside, I was still feeling a bit down from our trip to Pearl, so I said, 'Billy we need a drink,' "couldn't agree with you more" he said, so we headed across the road to the mall and a bar, it was here I first saw her, she was one of two hula dancers. We were standing on the second floor balcony looking down when our eyes met for the first time; she looked away and then straight back for a second look. I was still staring, I am sure I saw a little grin cross her face, I smiled back and gave her a wink and raised my glass as a salute, Billy and I stood there for about fifteen minutes, the day was catching up on us so we made a move back towards the hotel, better to be closer to home if your going to collapse through drink or fatigue.

Some time during the following afternoon I was out walking by myself, when I found I was out side a big shopping mall that Billy and me had visited the previous evening. The Hawaiian music was playing but the stage was empty, just my luck I thought to myself, no dancers. I was casually walking around looking in shop windows when I turned to be facing this beautiful girl in a Hawaiian grass skirt. "Will you dance with me?" she asked, it was the dancer from the previous night, I was stunned, I couldn't speak, "you can dance? I will show you" she said, 'dance here' I said. "Yes" she said, "I will show you," 'I don't think so, I have a very bad knee, but I will take you for a drink.' "When" she asked, I was taken back because I never expected that answer. 'What time do you finish?' I asked, "seven o'clock" she said, 'Where! and what time shall I meet you?' I asked. She pointed to a bar about fifteen feet away and said, "in there at nine thirty, my name is Alola, yours is? 'Johnny' I said, she smiled and then she was gone, was I dreaming or what, had I just been picked up by one of the most beautiful lest girls I had ever seen, was my luck really in?, well, I would see if she turns up at nine thirty. I think I walked around for the next hour or so in a trance, then slowly made my way back to the hotel, when I saw Billy I had to explain that our plans had changed for the night, and when I told him why he thought I was joking. 'Billy, I cant believe it myself mate, I still think I'm dreaming but I will know at nine thirty if I've had the piss taken out off me."

Nine o'clock I had showered, and spruced up with my best after shave, Billy said I smelt like a bloody fag (poof in English) but I felt good about myself so what the fuck. I arrived at the bar about twenty past nine, sitting there having a beer with a whisky and coke chaser, just to calm my nerves you understand, it was a nice bar as I remember, it had a couple of guys in the corner playing guitars, nice romantic Hawaiian stuff. It was about five to ten when I was thinking of pissing off, thinking I had been taken for a twat, when this voice said, hello Johnny, the smile melted all the anger that had just built up in me, 'hi' I said. "I'm so sorry I am late, it was difficult trying to get a cab." 'You're here now so there's no worries' I said, we sat drinking and talking for another hour and then she said she would show me the sights. I was happy just sitting there looking at her, she said she lived in a place called Kailua on the edge of a pineapple plantation, she had only worked in the city as a dancer for two months but its better than picking pineapples she said, she was twenty four years old but looked more like seventeen, she had a figure that some girls would die for, and men would climb over other women to get too.

We walked for about three quarters of a mile down the main street, when we came to a big old ware house, it was an all night Elvis convention, an Elvis Presley look alike met us on the door. "Welcome to my home folks, come in and look around, there's a lot of little mementoes you can buy and I will be only to glad to sign them for you." She had this wonderful little giggle, we walked and looked around for an hour or so but she wouldn't let me buy her anything, after being with her for a couple of hours it was as if we had known each other for sometime, we were so relaxed in each others company. Walking back towards the hotel along the beach we sat down on the sand for a rest, I took her hand and held it, she never pulled it away so I pulled her towards me, it was a kiss that started all my nerve ends tingling, I never wanted it to stop because it could only be followed with one thing and there's no way I was going to try my luck on the first night. 'I think we had better stop now' I said, "Yes, I think so too" she said. We walked back to my hotel where I was happy to see the car was still there. Billy and I had arranged to always leave the car keys in the hotel room's key cubbyhole, just in case one of us needed to use the car late at night or when we weren't together. As we reach the hotel door Alola said, "where are we going Johnny?" with a quiver in her voice, 'I'm taking you home you don't think I'm letting you go home by taxi this time in the morning do you, I've just got to get my car keys that are at the reception desk ok.' The smile returned and I didn't give a shit that I wouldn't get my leg over that night.

It was on the drive home to her place that she said she didn't have to work that day, so we could spend the whole day together. Kailua was nearly three quarters of an hours drive from Honolulu on the other side of the island, we arrived at a quaint little village on the out skirts of a small town, it was twilight and I couldn't make everything out properly but there was plenty of thatched huts around. I pulled over out side a shack that looked like it came straight out of Tom Sawyers casebook. She gave me directions how to get back the easy way as I had just come the scenic route. "It wont take so long it is main road all the way" she said, after kissing her again and holding her longer than I should have, I said I would meet her at midday down on the coast road, then I was off. I drove though the small town and hit the coast road, I turned right and followed the road all the way back to the Diamond Head, it didn't take so long to get home but I was in paradise, I had the sea on my left and rolling mountains on my right, and the smell of Alola in the car, I could easily have slept in the car but I thought better of it, I only had about four and a half hours sleep then I was up and met Billy for breakfast, he understood when I asked him if it was all right if I had the car for the day, "Don't make a mess in the back seat" he said with a smile on his face. 'I'll try and remember that' I said.

I was five minutes late but she was waiting where the road from town met the coastal highway, she had a basket in her hand, 'are we going somewhere?' I asked. "On a picnic, it's going to be a beautiful day" she said, and she was right, it was. I'm not going to put a number to how many times we made love, but every time was mind blowing, we would rest for a while play around in the sea then back at it again, eat a little, sunbathed a little, then back at it again, I remember one time when we were making love and she was sitting on me, I asked her if she could move her hip's like she does when she's dancing, "like this!" she said, 'STOP!' I shouted, I never had anything like it, boy that was something else, the last time we made love I was watching the sun go down over her shoulders, the sun made the ringlets of sweat on her back glisten, it definitely beat watching the sun set in the restaurant at Diamond Head, I was in paradise.

The picnic and the lady I will never forget.

The Rocks dad Rock Johnson

The following day Billy and I spent the day together, we drove along the coastal road all the way to Kaneohe Bay, and then cutting across country back to Pearl Harbour passing pineapple and mango groves on the way, we stopped a couple of times for fresh pineapple and coconut drinks, very refreshing. Rocky Johnson had phoned me that morning and asked if we would like to join him and his family for dinner that evening, we naturally and politely accepted his offer of a free nosh up, it was a nice drive up to Rocky's house, he lived in the north west of the island, a place called Aiea in a house that over looked the sea. On arrival we were invited to join the family in the swimming pool, trunks were then supplied and a cooling off period took place,

Rocky's son Dwayne must have took a liking to me, as it was me he wanted to drown by dive bombing me all the time, he was a fit little sod, he told me he was going to be a big football player when he grew up, well he tried, but it never materialized, to many injuries, so he followed his granddad and his Father into the wrestling game, and became known to the likes of you and me, as, THE ROCK. Saturday, the day of the fight, Billy and I went to the gym for a little circuit training, Billy trained each day for about an hour, but my training usually consisted of bending the elbow when lifting my glass, and waist and buttock movements when I was humping, mind you some would say that's the best exercise going.

We spent the rest of the day topping up our tans until it was time to go to the show,

We arrived at the stadium about six thirty and people were already going in although the show didn't start until eight forty five. After seeing the doctor and passing fit for the fight Billy and I took a short walk around the stadium, as we wasn't known it was all right, but as a rule wrestlers were not allowed to mix with the public in the halls or arena, villains and baby faces were not aloud to mix together ever in public, Billy and I were both baby faces and it was most unlikely that we would be wrestling each other anyway, as it happened I was wrestling another Englishman by the name of Les Thornton who had been out in the States for a number of years, if my memory serves me right I think one of the last times I saw Les was when we were working for Lew Phillips in Birmingham and that was back in the sixties, he left for the States in the seventies with other big names at the time, like Billy Robinson, Judo Al Hayes, Johnny Eagles, later to be followed Tony Charles, Chris Adams, Adrian Street, The Dynamite Kid, and Davy Boy Smith, that was one of the nice things about the wrestling game, if you were fortunate enough to travel, you never knew who you would meet up with around the world, it was like a few years after leaving England never to return I bumped into Johnny Eagles in Japan, where I reminded him of the last time we saw each other, it was in a shabeen in Brixton London, where I told him to keep his mouth shut, silly how some things you always remember about a person, John always had this big cheesy grin on his face and under the florescent lights his false teeth had turned pink.

Les had always been a stocky solid built person and he hadn't changed, the only thing now was he was Junior Heavyweight Champion of the World and was about to defend his title against me, this was going to be one hell of a good match. Two British wrestlers swapping holds, (it was nothing of the sort) Les had been out in the states so long that he forgot how to wrestle British style, don't get me wrong, what he did he did well, but it wasn't a British classic, the public seemed to like it and got excited in all the right places, the bout lasted twenty five minutes and I took the only fall to become World Junior Heavyweight Champion, I was ecstatic, full of myself, until I got back to the dressing room and was called into the promoters office. It started of like this. Well Mr Kincaid, and then I got the full politics of the

American wrestling game, I was brought back down to earth with a big bump, the only thing I came out of that bout with was sore elbows sore knees, rope burns and a bloody good pay packet, and a few photos of me with the strap, (Championship Belt), nothing else, the Belt had to stay in the States and I would have to go back to defend it, needless to say it never happened. Later that night Billy and I hit the town for the last time, we started off slowly but ended up more pissed than either of us had been on the three weeks we had been together, this was our last night so we made the most of it and no women were involved just two friends that might not see each other for a long time or may never see each other again, but that's life.

Unfortunately the promoter Peter Maivia died about five months later and I never did get another call to fight in Hawaii.

When I got back to England it would have been a waste of time telling the promoters that I was World Champion because they would have wanted to see the Belt, that I never had. Ok I earned a lot of money for that one bout but the politics of the wrestling game in America stinks. On my return from Hawaii I had a seven-week break before I was due back out to Beirut for a two-week tournament, so I decided to get in touch with Mr Hankestone the man from the brewery, he sounded quite shocked to hear from me, and he said in not so many words he didn't think he would, but he was glad that I did get in touch, I told him before we get to far in to this we had better talk because there is something I had to tell him. When we finally met up he was quite inquisitive, what was the urgency in my voice, so I proceeded to tell him about my previous convictions of G.B.H. and A.B.H. I also apologised for not telling him before, but said if we end up going to court for my licence and we got turned down because of my convictions, I didn't want him to feel stupid because he didn't know about them. I gave him a quick run down on what had happened for me to get the convictions in the first place, he smiled and said "leave it with me, I'm sure we can find a way around it, and in the mean time there's a pub we're reopening in Stevenage next week called The Long Ship, and if you don't mind I would like you and Jean to help out on the opening night and start your training thereafter." At this point I told him I still had a two-week contract to for-fill in Beirut, "not to worry" he said, "take it as an unpaid holiday." I was beginning to like this guy more and more, but I had a feeling not everything would be plain sailing. The next few days were hard, sorting out where the kid's would go and who was going to look after Bobby the dog.

TRAINING AT THE LONGSHIP

The following week we arrived at the Longship at eight thirty Wednesday morning and was greeted by a large lady who said she was the cleaner, she said the governor would be down shortly then she was gone, while we waited we took a look around, the refurbishment wasn't finished by a long way and by the look's of things the pub wouldn't be ready for opening by Friday, I could see the seating and the carpets had to be fitted and there was no pumps on the counter and nothing behind the bar, I was thinking to myself that they would be lucky to be finished in a fortnight, I was new in the game so what did I know, it was now nine o'clock and there wasn't a workman in sight, a door opened from beside the bar and a short stocky guy with a beard emerged, "hello" he said "you must be Johnny and Jean, I'm Danny and I'm your teacher for the next couple of weeks, I've been told you don't know the first thing about running a pub and we're starting from scratch, well I don't know fuck all myself so it will be the blind leading the blind", with that he let out a laugh that echoed all round the empty bar, "if only you could see your faces when I said that, they were a picture, your jaws just dropped" he said. "Well now that's broke the ice, lets go up stairs and have a cup of tea and meet the wife, and if you have any questions you can ask her, because your not get a straight answer out of me." His wife's name was Gill and she was at least six foot two inches tall and she had all the right curves in all the right places, I will tell you how I know in a moment.

After a cup of tea and a bit of breakfast Danny said to me, I hope you have brought some work clothes with you because we have a load of work to do in the engine room this morning (meaning the cellar), 'no problem mate just show me where we're staying and I'll get changed' I said. "Well that could be a problem, all the rooms have been painted and they still stink of paint, even we're not sleeping in any of the rooms, we sleep in the great hall along the corridor until the smell of paint goes, so my advice to you is, book in to a hotel, and put it down to the company, other wise you will wake up each morning with a bad head and puking everywhere." I took his advice and phoned a local hotel and booked Jean and me in for one week.

There was noise coming from down stairs so I guessed that the workmen had arrived, Danny asked if I wanted to go to the hotel now or help him in the cellar, I chose to stay and he pointed me in the direction of the hall and said I could get changed there. The pub was some size, it was a maze of doors, we had breakfast in the kitchen which was the size of a small house, along the corridor there were doors leading off to the toilets, too the down stairs bars, too the managers apartment, and too the live in staffs quarters, and of course too the great hall where I was about to make my entrance, I put my case on the floor and opened it. I took out my jeans and started to get undressed, I'd just dropped my trousers, believe it or not, but that's when I first noticed the very large four poster bed with silk curtains all around it at the other end of the hall, I stood very still not to make a noise, because behind those curtains was Gill, with the window behind her the sun shining in and she had just taken her dressing gown off, she must have been wearing a sheer silk or nylon night dress because it looked like she was wearing nothing, the silhouette was of a naked Amazon Goddess, I pulled my trousers up as fast as I could and got changed in the toilets, now that's not to say I didn't want to stay and ogle, it's just that it wouldn't have made a good impression on the first day if I'd got caught.

I knew a little about cellar work from what my mate Jim at the woodman pub had shown me, and Ken at the Bow Bell's. It was the real ales that was a cow son, spiking them and getting covered in beer, it's true what people say, learning the hard way is the best way and you learn much quicker, rotating the barrels and bottles, cleaning the beer lines and coca-cola, lemonade lines, making sure the gas bottles are secured or lying down, washing the cellar down and making sure the cellar is of the right temperature, oh, and making sure you have the right gas on the right beers, when I first started the

Guinness had its own gas in the barrel, and you would be surprised how many people took the head coupling of before releasing the gas, which the out come would be you get covered in Guinness, (been there done that got the tee-shirt).

We had to spike about three real ale barrels, Danny had a big smile on his face after we racked the last barrel, "do you want to spike the first barrel John?" he said. 'Now' I asked, "if you want" he said, so I walked over to the first barrel that we had racked put the peg in place and lifted the mallet, as I was about to tap the peg I heard Danny say "oh boy"! and as I turned to look at Danny there was this almighty gush of beer spouting up in the air, "get a peg in there quick" Danny shouted as he was laughing his bollocks off, he told me later he could see what I was going to do, I had raised the mallet about six to eight inches above the peg and there was no way that I would have pushed the peg in enough to stop the pressure of the gas pushing it back out, and it did and we lost nearly half the barrel by the time I got another peg in, I was covered in beer and I mean covered and he was still laughing when he said "do you want to spike the other's as your already wet.? 'Not on your fucking life mate you can piss off, I'm going for a shower' I said. After the shower Danny told me I could go and book in to the hotel but to be back at the pub about six o'clock, "have the rest of the day off and make the most of it, because you wont be getting much time of when we open" he said, I said thanks, picked up our case and left, I was in two minds to piss off back home because I didn't know if I could take this guy for two-weeks with out putting one on his chin. The Hotel was about ten minutes away from the pub on the other side of town, nothing flash but nice and comfortable,

Jean and I talked about the mornings work, I told her I was ready to fuck off home because I thought Danny was just a piss taker and it wouldn't be long before I put one on him, Jean said that she thought maybe he's just trying me out to see what temperament I had, was I quick to fly of the handle or could I hold my temper? I asked her, what made her think that?. Whilst Danny and I were down the cellar Gill told her David Hankestone had been to see them and talked a lot about me being a wrestler and being in trouble with the police, "putting two and two together, you did tell him about your convictions," it made sense, so I said, 'ok, we will give it our best shot.'

We arrived back at the pub around six o'clock, when we walked in I was amazed to see all the bench seating was in place, and there were pumps on the counter, when did all this happen I was wondering, in the corner stood new tables and chairs, at a rough guess I would say there were about twenty workmen doing one thing or another, Danny had just come up from the cellar carrying a crate when he saw me, "John just the man, help me carry these crates up then we can get busy filling the shelf's", just as well I was fit in those days because there was a bloody lot of crates, "how's your wrist action John", Danny asked. 'What do you mean Dan? Said I. "Are they strong, because we have about twenty optics to put up and there's two screws in each", 'that's ok, that will be twenty screws each,' I gave a little laugh, and so did he, we were going to get along fine.

When we finished bottling up the shelf's Danny said, "dinner should be ready shortly so we had better go and get washed up." Jean had been helping bottle up as well so we were all a bit on the dirty side. When Gill called us for dinner Danny had just finished putting the last screw in the last optic, "now that's what you call coming together" Danny said, did everything have to be about sex with this guy, or was it all in my mucky mind? After dinner we all sat down to comfy drinks and a chat, Danny told us how he got into the pub game via the buses, he was a driver and Gill was a conductor, you had to see these two together to appreciate what I was thinking, there's Danny who stands about five foot eight, and there's Gill who happened to be six foot one Amazon, I just couldn't imagine her walking along saying fare's please, (I had a vision of someone saying to her piss, off I'm not paying, and her retaliating with, give me your fucking money or I'll break your fucking arm). I was sitting there smiling to myself when Danny said, "what's so funny? let us in on the joke." How could I tell him what I was thinking, so I just said, 'I was thinking, I always wanted to drive a bus, maybe if this don't work out I'll try it,' I don't think he believed me but he let it go.

Danny told us about the pub and the reputation it had before it closed for the refurbishment, it was a rough house, fight's nearly every night, and it was his (stroke,) our job to turn it around, meaning if any of the idiots come in and start trouble it was our job to evict them, ask them to leave nicely and not to come back. "Do we have any doormen?" I asked. "The brewery look down on doormen, as people see doormen and think it must be a trouble pub to warrant them, so no doormen are employed in any of their pubs, he said. 'This could make for one hell of a busy night I said, so I think we had better get an early night, do you think the pub will be ready for opening on time?, I asked. "There's only the carpets and the pool table's to come in, it will all be up and running by four o'clock when the governors arrive for their free drink's, then we open to the public at six o'clock" he said. I thanked them for the dinner and the drink's, and said we would be back at nine o'clock sharp in the morning, to start the first day of my new career.

Friday the 15th of April 1983 was the day I started my new career as assistant manager of a public house, and it's a day that I will never forget, for a few reasons, when we opened the doors to let the company representatives in, there were a load of managers from various pubs as well, they all came to see (so they said) what the new refurbishment looked like, but you soon find out they just came for the free drinks,

Jean had been upstairs all day helping Gill do the food for the opening, which never lasted long once it was brought down, it was as if they hadn't eaten for a week, the greedy bastard's.

Most of the office wallers made a bee line for me and asked me how it was going, and was I missing the wrestling, and had I met Mick McManus or Jackie Pallo?, I thought, what the fuck's going on here, have they come to see how the company have spent their money doing the place up, or have they come to quiz me on wrestling.

Thank God the big wig's never stayed to long, but the rest of the pub governors were putting the drink down as if it was going out of fashion, as I got more into the pub trade I realised why the pub managers were like that, you see the brewery are not known for giving much away, so when there's a reopening of a pub and the brewery is footing the bill, you eat and drink as much as you can on them, even that came to an end when the brewery got wise to what was happening.

Most of the pub managers were pissed by half five and were calling for cab's, how half of them ran their pub's I don't know, Danny and I got busy clearing up and getting ready to open to the public, Danny took me by the arm and walked me behind the counter and said "have a look under there" pointing to a shelf next to the sink, as I bent I could just see the handle of a baseball bat sticking out, "that's only used in dire emergency's you understand, meaning if there are more than one or two people on top of me and you don't think you can get them off! use it, as I would for you, ok,?" he said, "Ok, but will it get that rough?" I said. "Hopefully not, as long as we watch each others back we should be alright", he said. Now was he saying this to wind me up?, because if he was, he was doing a great job of it.

Every thing was going along fine until about nine o'clock when some arsehole decided to have a beer fight, Danny was over there double quick, and I heard him say to the lad in question, we only had this carpet laid this afternoon and it's not nice you throwing beer all over it, so please refrain from doing so or I will have to ask you to leave, all this without raising his voice to loud.

Why is it when you speak to someone in a pleasant tone they have to take you for a prick? "Piss off, it's only a carpet" the guy said with aggression in his voice. "Yeh! my carpet" Danny said as his fist connected perfectly with mouth Almighty's jaw, he was out before he fell back onto his seat, Danny turned to the other lad and said "I'm not barring you because you had the decency to realise you were in the wrong and didn't mouth it off, but I never want to see his face in here again, so please take him out and take him home," the guy was just coming round when his friend picked him up and half carried him out.

Danny turned to see me standing about five foot away from him, he gave me a wink and walked towards me, and as he passed me he said, "that's how it's done, it's your turn next"

Some time later it was my turn, a couple of lad's round by the pool table were arguing about something and getting very loud, "what's wrong lads"? I enquired, "What's it got to do with you"?. fuck off. "I don't think so my old son" I'm the assistant manager and if I can sort it out for you I will, but all your doing right now is drawing "attention to yourself". "Isn't your hearing to good pal?. "I told you to fuck off", as he stuck his face in mine. Well anybody who knows me, would know that's not the smartest thing to do, our friend was out before he hit the floor, I turned to the other guy and said 'do you have a problem with that,' he shook his head, so I told him to leave the area, I knelt down to help silly bollocks up, but he didn't want my help and tried to push me away, some people never learn, before his hand actually touched me his arm was up his back, I had grabbed his hair and wrenched his head back so he was looking at the ceiling, and walked him slowly though the crowd to the door, once through the door I let him go, and stood back a few paces, 'now my friend, you want to fight me, be my guest, but I'll tell you now, I won't be as gentle as I was in there, and before you start throwing all the verbal at me, I'm not barring you, you wont be allowed back in tonight but the next time you come in, you play by our rules, does that seem fair to you?,' he looked at me for a while nodded, turned and left.

Back in the bar Danny was standing behind the door, "I liked it, but will he behave the next time he's in" asked Danny, 'well if he don't, I will introduce him to pain and he wont be coming back again' I said. "Let's get a drink, the next one's mine" Danny said. As it happened there was no more trouble that night, the atmosphere seemed to have changed for the better, everybody was chatty and friendly and when time was called they drank up and left with out a fuss, my first night was over and I didn't even pull a pint, not until we had closed that was, then we sat down with the staff to discuss any problems they had during the night, (minor problems with the customers, or workings of the till.)

Over the next four day's Danny pointed out to me one staff member that was on the fiddle (taking money from the till). When he eventually called this person into the office he wanted me there as well, just to note the procedure, he never allowed any of his staff to carry money when they were on duty, so if they had money on them at the end of a shift it had to come from the till. Danny had some one watch this particular person all night and just before closing time he called her into the office and blatantly called her a thief. "You have been taking money from my till for the last four day's and now I want you to empty all your pockets", she refused to comply, so Danny picked up the phone and said "you either turn out your pockets or I call the police, now", reluctantly she empted her pocket and produced fifteen pounds, "now the rest" Danny said. "That's it, that's all I have," she said. "Would you like my wife down here to search you or should I call the police? With that she gave a sigh, stuck her hand down her bra and came out with sixty pounds in twenty pound notes, she had worked every night since we opened, and every night was busy, so Danny said "I'm sorry love but I have to call the police, if you have been averaging seventy odd pounds a night over the last four nights you have stolen over two hundred and eighty pounds, not even a fool would allow that, and I'm no fool" he said, with that Danny phoned the police. Gill had now come into the office, Danny turned to me and said "the bar's closed John will you get the pub emptied and buy the staff a drink, I would like to talk to them in a short while."

After the police had gone, Danny came and sat with us, he had a face on I hadn't seen before, he started with, "boys and girls, I had to do something that I really hated doing tonight, and that's call the police in because somebody was thieving, not a little but a lot, she took me for a mug and I'm nobody's mug, now if anybody else is at it, my advice is to stop now, if any of you are in any kind of financial difficulties come and see me and I will lend you the money, but don't nick it out of my till's." He got up as abruptly as he sat down and left the bar without saying good night to anybody. 'He's really pissed off, but so would I be if I had to pay back three hundred pounds that was stolen' I said.

I remember the following day at breakfast when Danny brought up the happenings of the previous night, he said "Johnny did you learn anything from last night?" giving me a side ways look as he stuffed a piece of bacon in his mouth. 'Such as' I asked, "such as, never do an interview with a member of staff alone, especially when your accusing one of theft, and always speak with a calm tone in your voice it makes you sound more confident of what your talking about, as if your not guessing, but defiantly know what's been going on, and last but not least, always threaten them with the police, normally that will always turn the table in your favour."

'I thought the chat to the staff was very moving, an Oscar winning performance the way you came in with a look of thunder on your face, then gave a stern speech and left, they had never seen you like that before, I think it got the message across that you can be a nice guy, but not to be fucked with, or else,' Danny winked at me. "Is that the way you saw it?" he asked. 'Yes, that's the way I saw it,' I said. "Not bad, your quick at reading people, always make the staff think that your their best friend, and in a week or two you will find out the ones who are here to rip you off, because they think your easy, then when you catch them have them nicked, and show your staff the other side of your face, now, if nobody resigns by the following Friday you have a good set of staff, but if they do, it means they were here for what they could take, comprende?"

I understood all right, because two nights later one of the guys phoned in and said he wouldn't be coming back, and gave some stupid reason.

Danny said he would teach me all he could within the short time we have together, and if only a quarter of the stuff he teaches me gets though, it's a quarter more than I had in the first place.

We stayed with Danny and Gill for a week and a half, then Jean and I were moved on to another pub in Luton called The Biscuit Mill.

THE BISCUIT MILL

It was while Jean and I was doing our training at the Biscuit Mill, she came to me one lunch time and said, "your not going to Beirut" and I asked her 'why not? "They have just blown up the American Embassy" she said. 'Is that all?, I'm British not American' I said. I was still determined to go. About five day's later she came to me again, "your defiantly not going" she said. 'Where' I asked. "To Beirut" she said. 'And why's that? I asked, "They have just blown up the British Embassy" she said. 'I'm not going' I said,

The rest of the lads that were booked on the same trip as me, decided to go, and after the first show, the stadium was hit by a mortar bomb, and they were all sent home with a fortnights basic money. I could have kicked myself for not going, but sometimes it's better to be safe than sorry.

Beirut was supposed to have been my last International wrestling trip abroad, and it was! for a few years, but we will come to that later.

We were training at the Biscuit Mill for just under two weeks, nothing much happened there, we just learned a bit more company paper work, and the manager taught us the law's concerning the pub trade, the manager was to me a financial wizard with money, he just looked at a column of figures and wrote the answers down, with me it was a calculator job, no calculator no job.

David Hankestone the area manager came to see Jean and I, and said he was giving us the rest of the week off, as he would like us to take over the Bow Bells the following Monday, it was like giving me a electric shock, I tingled all over, the thought of getting my own pub at last, then you start to worry, am I ready, do I know enough, will I be able to handle it? then I thought, fuck it, be positive, if I fuck up, I wouldn't be the first one to have dropped a bollock. So Jean and I finished work on the Tuesday night, the manager wished us well, and said if I ever got stuck on anything to give him a call first, and he will do his best to set it right, I thanked him and told him I had appreciated all that he had shown us, and hope to do him proud in the future. "I'm sure you will" he said, as he waved us good by.

THE BOW BELL

Monday morning at ten o'clock I had to meet David Hankestone outside the Magistrate's Court in Fenny Stratford, this was to see if I would get my licence for the running of the Bow Bell. I asked David if he had informed the licensing officer of my previous convictions and he said he had, the licensing officer also said that if we don't mention the convictions, neither would he, because the Bow Bell needed someone like me in there, someone they could look up to, and would keep control, (now I was getting the bullshit,) I said 'David, don't you mean if they take the piss or fuck up in some way, I wouldn't stand for any crap, and you would be right? Lets not fuck about with each other lets call a spade a spade, if I whack someone will I have the police on my back? "If, as you say whack someone, as long as you don't send them to hospital I don't think the police will bother you, if a complaint is put in then they will have to investigate, but I can assure you they wont investigate too hard, but its unlikely that anyone would put in a complaint, as you know, the estate has a bad reputation and they don't like the police coming on to it."

I was called into the witness box about ten forty five, now I don't know about you! but every time I have gone into a witness box I am as nervous as hell, I am sure there going to find me guilty of something, its only when I have finished reading the card (I swear by almighty God that the evidence I shall give is the truth the whole truth and nothing but the truth) that I start to get the shakes, I think its because in all my court cases I have always been found guilty, except for once.

After fifteen or twenty minutes, and after the chairman and his sidekicks have had their little chat he turned to me and said, "ok Mr Kincaid licence granted you can leave the box now." "Thank you" I said.

I left that courthouse with one big cheesy grin on my face; I was like the cat that got the cream, until we arrived back at the Bow Bell that is. The removal lorry was out side the pub and Ken and Pauline were seeing their furniture and belongings in. Inside Jean was sitting at the counter with a hot cup of tea, she had already done a cash check and signed the change over, I had dropped her of at the pub before going to court, we had already arranged for our furniture and belonging to be delivered the following day, as we only lived ten minutes away from the pub, and it would have been too much to move our belongings in and open the pub at the same time.

Well, the time came when Ken came to me and said, "the lorry's all packed and the cats in the car, and we are ready to go, there's only one thing left to do, and that's to give you these keys, and say, its all yours mate, and good luck."

I was shaking, the last time I felt like this was when I was about to have my first professional fight, I was close to making a mess in my pants, I thought the worst is yet to come, I have to face the punters, and try to remember everything that Ken told me about certain people.

Opening time was approaching and surprisingly I was feeling quite calm as if I had been doing this for years, it's hard to explain the feeling, but it was as if somebody had taken all the worry away from me, and I was beginning to look forward to opening the doors.

The date was 19 of May 1983, and I was about to open the doors of my first official pub, I was a bit apprehensive but then who wouldn't be, I had less than four weeks training for this career move, and I should have been shitting myself, but my nerves held as I unlocked and slipped the bolts on the door for the first time.

The first person in greeted me with, "you're late,"'no, I'm John' I said, and your lucky I'm open at all,' because at this precise time I had no staff and didn't know if any were coming in or not, a couple of minutes later the bar maid came rushing through the doors shouting, "sorry I'm late, and I haven't got an excuse." 'I'm glad about that I said; because there's nothing worse than hearing a lot of old shit that's probably lies anyway,' she looked at me and smiled, "and top of the morning to you too," she said. She stood about five foot five, slim with shoulder length hair, not big busted, but all the right curves in the right places, a very nice natured girl and she had a lovely soft Irish accent. 'The till is in and switched on I said; now I have something to do out the back, if you need anything, give me a shout.' To tell you the truth I had nothing to do but my nerves were starting to get the better of me, I couldn't just stand there and watch the punters come in one by one and greet them, I can handle a crowd much better than one or two, so I went and sat in the office for about half an hour, and organised it the way I wanted it, everybody has their own way of having things in their office so I sat there and rearranged every thing to suite me, (what a load of crap,) I just wanted something to keep me occupied so I didn't have to be out front,

After a good length of time, and by the noise coming from the bar area, we were starting to get busy, the time had come to show myself, so I left the safety of my office and walked through the bottle cellar towards the bar, just before entering the bar I put my best smile on and opened the door, the first face I was greeted with was Phyllis. "Hello governor mines half of Guinness" she said, and before she could get another word out, I said 'and your paying for this one love.' "Yes I am, and would you like one as well" she asked. Thank you, 'I will join you in a half of Guinness if that's ok.' I looked along the bar and it seemed that everybody had a beer in front of them so I lifted the hatch and walked slowly over to where Phyllis had sat down with my half of Guinness. 'It's nice to see a friendly face on my first day' I said. "Don't worry" she said; "they will all be friendly, just to see how far they can go with you, then you will see their true faces, it may take a week or two, but you will make up your own mind which ones you can trust and which ones you cant, I'm not going to tell you to watch this one or that one, it's up to you to sort the who's who out, and if you cant, there's going to be a lot of trouble in this pub, and that's all I've got to say" 'Thanks I said you've been a great help.' "We'll see" was her reply. A small crowd started to gather by the ladies toilets at the end of the bar, between the end of the bar and the toilets stood the fag machine, with all these bodies around it you couldn't see it, so one of the first thing I would have to do is move it, take temptation of robbing it out of the way, I remembered the previous governor telling me it had already disappeared once, I thanked Phyllis for the drink and stepped back behind the bar, I was making my way slowly to the end where the crowd had gathered, passing a couple of old fellows standing at the bar. 'Good afternoon gentlemen' I said. One looked at me and the other one replied, "after-noon governor, so you're the new man are you, how long do you intend staying for? He enquired." 'I haven't moved any of my stuff in yet, so lets see what to day brings shall we, but I do like a good challenge,' I said. He smiled gave me a wink and offered his hand, as I took it he said, "I think you and I are going to get along, my name is John he said and so is my friends," I smiled and said 'well that makes three of us. 'Can I buy you a drink gentleman as it's my first day, and I'm in a generous mood, it may never happen again. Little John ordered a pint of Guinness and big John had a whisky. 'I can see this getting very confusing when I call one of you, I said. The big one spoke for the first time, with a broad Glaswegian accent, he said; "I'm known as Rhodesian

John, and the wee man is John Morrison he runs the sweetshop across the square, he knows everything and everybody, and as for me if you need any work done I'm your man." 'Well what can I say to that' I said, it was a pleasure meeting you two and I'm sure we will behaving many a drink together.

I moved on to the end of the counter where a lot of bodies were looking at me, a couple of them piped up with polite conversation while a couple of them tried there hard man stare on me, you know the look, clenching of the teeth, making the jaw muscle twitch, the intimidating look, there was one guy in particular who wouldn't take his eyes of me and he had this look, I let it go for a while then I had to say something, I called him closer to the bar and asked him if he had a problem with me and if he did there was one of two things he could do about it, one was to leave the bar and not come back because I'm here to stay, or we could go outside and see who walks back in first, if you get my meaning, he said he didn't know what the fuck I was on about, the mans bottle had gone, and he never looked at me that way again, well not that I saw anyway.

Over the next few days more and more faces were coming in, some I sensed I would have trouble with, they came in from the pub next door which was less than a hundred and fifty yards away called (The London Pride), they came in mainly to try and wind me up, well one fat guy succeeded in doing so, as I came out of the cellar one night there was this fucking great Bowie Knife stuck in the counter, 'I asked who owns that,' and the fat lump said he did, 'take it out and put it away'

I said. "And if I don't?" he asked. 'I'll take it out and stick it as far up your arse as it will go, and if you don't think I can, leave it there until I come round.' With that I started to walk down the length of the bar to the hatch way, by the time I reached the fat man the knife had gone and out of sight, I said, 'now you can fuck off, because twats like you I just don't need in here,' he stood there looking at me for at least five seconds and decided I wasn't about to back down, so he made the right move and left the premises.

Most of the guys down the London end were characters, Phil the Cab, Tom the Painter, Ginger John, Ron the Bread, One eye Chris, John the Tape,

Barry, Dickie, Eric, Jimmy Castle, and the Whitley Brothers, Alan, John, & Jimmy!

There were also a few characters at the other end of the bar, the pool end or the Scottish end, as it was known. One such character was a guy called Alan, he had a deep Glaswegian accent and he was very loud, when he laughed you could hear him in the next building, I'm sure the first time I spoke to him was in the men's toilets, he asked me if I was really the new governor, and when I told him I was he said, "look mate it's not that I'm prejudice but your not going to turn this into a black pub are you?" I smiled at him and winked, as he washed his hands and was about to leave I said to him "I like to be in the minority, so I think we will leave it as it is." He said "you big black bastard you had me worried then" and gave me one of his hearty laughs, he shook my hand and said, "welcome to the Bow Bells."

Later that night Alan called me over to his table to introduce me to his wife, he said "Mini this is the big black bastard," again he had a bloody great grin on his face, 'why do you keep calling me that, I asked, knowing full well that he definitely wasn't prejudice because his wife was an Indian. "You never told me your name" he said, "you are a big black person, I don't mean anything rotten when I call you a bastard it's just a word, and I mean it in a friendly way. We have been the closest of friends since that time.

Mini was about to drop her second child, and Alan had no way of getting her to the hospital. I asked him how much had he had to drink and he said one pint, why? I threw him the keys to my B.M.W and said get her to the hospital now. The following day he came in to the pub and announced he was a father of a wee little girl.

I had never seen the big Scotch twat looking more proud, and since 1983 he still calls me the three B's.

There was also a few women characters, like Big Cass Williams, hard as nails but with a heart of gold, she wouldn't think twice of having a go at a fella, but when it came to kid's she couldn't do enough for them, she organised all the kid's parties, and we did have a lot of kid's parties, but to crown it all she told me she loved kid's because she was brought up in a home and she never had a lot. I enquired which home she was brought up in as I was in a home when I was a kid. "Beacholme," she said, "It's in Banstead Surrey." 'I know that' said I 'because that's the very place I spent my last days at school, I was in Beacholme for the last three and a half years before I left school.' "You're shitting me" she said. 'I'm not' said I. "I was in Maple house before they moved me to Larch house." She screamed and said she was in Cedar house next door to Larch, Cass is three years older than me so it's unlikely that we would have known each other there but it's such a coincidence that two Beacholme kid's end up thirty odd years later living on the same Estate in Milton Keynes.

There was another girl on the Estate, Miss C who used the pub and thought she was hard, but basically she was just a fucking bully, if she could intimidate a person she would, but the less said about her the better.

At the end of the first week, Sunday night, I was sitting in my office doing the paper work and counting the money, when I found I was three hundred and something pounds short, panic set's in, so I counted the money again, and again it came up short, I checked the paper work again, the paper work came out the same as before, I checked the money again, bollocks it's still short, now I'm starting to think where it could have gone, have I brought anything and not put a receipt in, no, who's been in the office, could they have got in the safe, I don't know, I am now sweating, were could it have gone?. I thought, leave it and check it in the morning that was the wrong move, because I couldn't sleep all night worrying about it. First thing Monday morning I was back in that office counting notes again, and again it was short, I could think of only one thing to do and that was phone Tom from the Biscuit Mill, he said, don't panic and he would be down within the hour. It was easy for him to say it wasn't his three hundred and odd pounds missing. That was the longest hour I have ever waited. When he arrived I showed him into the office and showed him the paper work, he asked me if I had brought anything and I assured him I hadn't, he told me to piss off and leave him with it and he would give me a shout later, fifteen minuets later he called me into the office, "ok John he said what have you been buying? "Nothing I said, I even asked Jean if she had taken money to buy anything without telling me and she said she hadn't." "It's in the safe he said. 'What's in the safe?' I asked. "The bloody money" he said. 'Where' I said. "Try counting the change and not just the notes and you might come up with the right figure" he said, you forgot the pound coins and the 50p, 20p, 10p, 5p, and the copper, your trying to hard he said, take your time, the paper work is ok it's normally the other way around, people fuck up on the paper work and the cash is way out, by the way your twenty six pence over in your safe, well done.

At the end of my second week I had my official pub opening night. I had invited some of my friends from the world of wrestling down to celebrate the opening with me, names like Catweasel, Johnny Kwango, Lee Bronson, Dave Butcher Bond, Iron Fist Clive Myers, Sid Cooper.

The official opening was to start at around seven o'clock p.m. At five o'clock I had the governor in from the pub next door, and we were having a nice sociable drink and a laugh with my guests, then five of the bosses from the brewery turned up with my area manager, I also had two of my relatives staying with me, my mothers brother Keith and his wife Christine. At seven o'clock when we opened the doors you would have thought we were the only bar open in Milton Keynes, they came from every direction. I have never seen a bar get so full so quick, I had three bar staff working, myself and Jean, and my uncle Keith, even Mickey the governor from the bar next door helped for about fifteen minutes, then with a wave of his hand he shouted "see you later" and he was gone,

We had a duet up on the high level, a guitarist and a drummer, not that you could hear them, when everybody had their drinks and it quietened down a bit, I introduced my colleagues to the customers, Catweasel and Kwango were the stars, if they had charged for there autographs they would have made a small fortune, along time ago Gary (Catweasel) used to play in a jazz band as a drummer, so up he goes and takes over the drums, he did a five minute drum solo, the guy was magic and so thought all my punters as well, the atmosphere inside the pub was unbelievable, it was as you say! Jam-packed, and there was not one bit of trouble. I had a late licence until a quarter to twelve, and the Bow Bell being the Bow Bell the police were around dead on twelve o'clock to make sure there were no late drinks being served, and everybody was leaving the pub. One of the officers tapped Kwango on the shoulder and asked him to drink up, as Johnny turned to face him the shock showed on the officers face, his jaw dropped, then he said, "aren't you Johnny Kwango?" "That's right son" he said, "I'm sorry but my dad is a big fan of yours, do you think I could have your autograph for him?," Johnny gave him one of his toothy smiles and got him to hold his beer while he signed his autograph, later he told me he had signed my signature instead of his own, that's what we used to do when we were tagging together, he would sign my name and I would sign his, we had over a hundred and thirty tag-matches together, Kwang was like a dad to me.

When we eventually closed the doors we were all knackered, the area manager said " "Mr Kincaid, I have never seen this pub with so many people in, and there wasn't a single fight, to be fair, it would have been kind of stupid for anybody to start a fight knowing the kind of people you had visiting you tonight," then he went on to say, "I think this pub is going to be to small for you," he then shook all the guys hands and thanked them for coming and supporting me, he said to Catweasel, he enjoyed his drum playing but he's so glad that he had turned his hand to wrestling, because he gave him and his kids so much enjoyment, he looked at Kwango and said "I wont forget your face my friend," Kwangs answer was "not many people do."

Unfortunately Kwango and Catweasel are no longer with us, they were two guys one could never forget, and one wouldn't want to.

The following morning Mickey the governor from the pub next door came in, he looked shagged out, "when are you having another one of those" he said, "I'm not" said I, "thank fuck for that, I only had one bar staff on last night, and who couldn't get in here came to my place, I've never taken so much money and I've never worked so fucking hard." Mickey still mentions that night when I see him.

From International Wrestler to Pubs and Punters

One or two days later I was collecting glasses up on the high level when I approached this couple sitting there on the long bench seat, "after-noon" I said, "good after-noon" said the chap "are you the new governor here" he enquired, "I am" said I, "do you mind if I shag my girl on this seat" he asked, I was taken back, I was stunned, there was this lovely well dressed lady and a guy who spoke very well asking if he could fuck his women on my furniture, "yes I do" said I, "use the floor you might make a mess on my seat," with an almighty great laugh he offered his hand and said "I like you and I think I have found my hole in the wall," I didn't get the meaning of that at the time, but he came in once or twice a week, some times with the lady, but more often than not with two or three guys, they were always well dressed and well spoken, in fact a lot of my customers thought they were old bill, (police) so I had to make enquires of my new friend, because I didn't want to lose my main trade just because I had police drinking in there, my new friend ensured me that they were defiantly not old bill, they were council workers, and as he didn't have an office as such he invited them along to the pub and conducted his business over a pint, we became very close friends over the years.

It wasn't till I was there a month or so that I got to know who the bullies were, who were the thief's and who were the cat burglars, as it was pointed out to me cat burglars are not like the common thief, common thief's nick of anybody, cat burglars nick of people who are insured, (meaning rich people) stores and shops, I had no time for the thief's and tried to discourage them from using the pub, they would break in to a house nick what they could, giving no thought to the people they were nicking from, it didn't matter if they didn't have a pot to piss in or a penny to there name, then what ever they nicked they thought they could come into the pub and try and flog it, if I saw this going on, and I did catch a few, they would be out the door double quick, and they new it, even the so called villains didn't want these scum bags in the pub and pointed them out to me.

The pub had a pool team, and men's and ladies dart teams, so it was a fairly sporty pub, The pool team was riding high in the league, and the ladies dart team was up there as well, but the men's dart team was completely shit, apparently they only played for a night out on the booze and a bit of fun.

At this point I think I had only played pool once before, but I was quite taken with the game, I used to watch this black guy by the name of Horace, he was shit hot, he would swerve the ball to the left, then swerve it to the right, make it come back to him, follow through hit the cushions and then come back to him, I was mesmerised watching him perform, I got him to show me how he made these shots and when I closed the bar at night I would practice, at first I couldn't do it, I tried and I tried but my cue would just keep slipping off the cue ball, I would practice for hours but it would just keep slipping off, until finely one night watching me he said "try chalking the fucking cue you plonker," you know it's amazing what a little bit of chalk can do, and how much it can cost you, the pool machine was only twenty pence back then, but it cost me a small fortune to practice after closing, all because I never used a piece of chalk, It took a while but eventually I got into the pool team, at first I was only used as a substitute but as my game got better I was playing in the team regularly.

The so called estate hard man started to use the pub on a regular basis all though he mostly drank in the pub next door with his family, I expect this was to see how I ran things, but then one of his monkey friends started coming in with him and they started to become a nuisance, one night I was doing my rounds socialising when I had just past the dyed bleached haired plonker, he was having a go at this guy who was considerably a lot smaller than him, and he was being very loud, "keep it down a bit lads" I said, "fuck off," he said without turning and looking at me, 'no, if anyone's going to fuck off its going to be you,' he then turned and with a lot of aggression in his voice he said "fuck off," it took one punch, and before he hit the deck I was already looking at his pal and was about to say, be my guest, when he put his hands in the air and said nothing to do with me, and walked away, I picked the mouthy twat up and walked him to the door on shaky legs, one of the London end boys said now you have to watch yourself John, because he is a dirty fighter, what he can't do in front of you he will do behind your back, fuck me , within minutes of him telling me that an ex-barman walked out of the side door, then walked back in backwards, when he turned around he had another mouth on his forehead, apparently one of the lads at the other end of the bar saw the twats mate take a pool cue out, and him thinking it was me coming through the door took a swing, but the wrong guy got it.

After I ran the injured party to hospital to get stitched up, I went looking for the twat and his mate because I didn't fancy being ambushed like the barman was, it's funny, but for a so called hard-man and a sneaky side-kick they were hard to find, I looked everywhere for them except their houses, I never take trouble to some ones door, that's my moral standing, unless they bring it to me or my family first, to cut a long story short it was about six weeks before I saw either of them again, and not a word was said.

Not a lot happened in the five months I stayed at the Bow Bell, one or two staff changes, one or two boy's got put away, but that was about it.

Roger and Jill from the Bletchley Arms were leaving to take over there own pub, and the area manager asked me if I would like to take over the Bletchley Arms, he said it was big enough to suit my needs, so I agreed to give it a bash, now Roger wasn't happy about this and tried to put me off, he wouldn't give me a specific reason for not wanting me to take it, he just kept saying it's not the pub for you, I should have known that he wouldn't put me wrong, because when we were at the Bow Bells Jean and I never had a day off in the first three months and it was beginning to get to us, bickering and arguing with each other over nothing, Roger asked when we last had a day off and I said we hadn't had one yet, he said "are you mad, you must take a day off or you will drive each other crazy, next Wednesday your taking your wife out for a meal and I'm going to look after your pub for you, is that understood," what could I say to that! Except "thanks," that night was like taking a week off, and a big weight being lifted from my shoulders,

From International Wrestler to Pubs and Punters

It was while I was at the Bow Bell's that my wrestling promoter from Birkenhead, Liverpool, phoned and said that he had a letter for me from the Salvation Army, sent care of Brian Dixon Wrestling Enterprise, I was intrigued, not being too religious I wondered what the Salvation Army wanted with me, I told Brian to send it to me, and I waited on it's arrival, When it finally arrived and I opened it, it was from the Investigation Department Salvation Army, stating that they had a David Kincaid on there book's who was looking for his father, who happens to be a professional wrestler, and if they have contacted the wrong person they are sorry for any inconvenience they might have caused. It took the wind right out of my sail's, I had a feeling that one day this would happen, you try and prepare yourself for it, but it doesn't matter how much you try, your never prepared.

I lost my son when he was three years old, his mother moved house without telling me, and told her parents not to tell me where she had gone, I tried for a short while to find them, but for all I knew, they could had gone back to Scotland where she was originally from, I was wrestling up and down the country at the time, so maybe she would see my name on a poster and have a change of heart and bring him along to see me, it never happened, I was told years later that she did see my name on a wrestling poster once, but crossed the road quickly so David never saw it, even her parents said she was out of order, and would try to persuade her to change her mind, but at the end of the day they would have to abide by her ruling, it was fifteen years later when the letter from the Sally Army dropped through my letter box,

I promptly telephoned the number that would put me in touch with someone that had the information that I craved, only to be told that they would give me another telephone number of a social worker who worked on David case, who in turn gave me another number of the place where David lodged, I took my phone in hand again and rang the number given to me, this very polite voice on the other end enquired who I was after, I said 'David Kincaid, I'm his father' the voice got very excited and said they would run along and get him and he would phone me back in ten minuets, I didn't have ten minuets, I had to go and pick my daughter up from school, but the phone was already dead, it took me close on half hour to get too and from the school, as I came in Jean said David had phoned and he will be calling back in fifteen minuets, but just in case he left a number for you, Jean went on to say she thought it was me phoning, messing about, as he sounded just like me, I couldn't wait for the call so I dialled the number that he left, I was speechless the voice on the other end was a mans voice, the last time I spoke to David he was only three years old, I choked, the first words he said to me was, Hello Dad, I wanted to speak but nothing came out for at least twenty five seconds, and then Jean had to feed me, ask him who he looks like she said, so I did, the answer was, "I have an old photo of you, my hairs not as tight as yours, my skin colouring is a little lighter than yours, but I look more like you than mum," great I thought to myself, 'how tall are you' I asked, "six foot one and a half" came the reply, 'fuck me, I'm just a midget' I said, "I know mum told me" he said, and we both gave a hearty laugh. "When can I come and see you?" he asked, 'whenever you want,' he came straight back with "would tomorrow be alright," 'tomorrows fine by me' I said.

The following day I was working in my office when Mandy my step Daughter came in and said, "He's here," "great, I'll be out in a couple of minuets" said I, it took another ten minutes and another visit from Mandy before I could muster enough courage and composure to front my son, does that sound daft, I didn't know the boy, I didn't know anything about him, his like's, his dislike's, I felt scared, apprehensive, yet he was my son, so what had I got to worry about, as I opened the cellar door and entered the bar he was standing right in front of me, it was like looking at myself twenty two years prior, I walk around the bar without taking my eyes of off him, as I approached him I put out my hand and he came straight in for a bear hug, we hugged for a good couple of minuets and we both were whimpering like a couple of snivelling babies, I said "lets go round the back or my street cred will be blown to bit's," we sat in my office for about ten minuets when David said his social worker brought him down and we have left him standing at the bar, we were both laughing when we entered the bar area, and his social worker had a relieved smile on his face.

Slowly I found out more and more about how David was brought up, it wasn't so dissimilar to the way I was, in and out of homes, foster parents, then into lodgings when he was old enough to fend for himself, it wasn't surprising that he had a slight chip on his shoulders, I know I did when I left the home and went into a youth hostel, then into lodging when I was sixteen, I was jack the lad, I thought the world owed me something for all the shit I was put through, but I came through it, and I was sure David would all so,

Everybody deals with things there own way, David had to challenge everything and everybody, even me, I'm not saying that's a bad thing as long as it's done with the right attitude, but David had to be right, and if you questioned what ever, you could feel the aggression coming through, there was a very angry young man inside of him that wanted to come out, in the early days when he used to visit he always came down with a couple of friends, it started of with lets arm wrestle Dad, and he would keep on until I arm wrestled him, at this I wasn't the best, but I wasn't the worse either, I learnt a lot off Clive Myers (Ironfist), he showed me a lot of different techniques as at the time he was still Lightweight Arm-Wrestling Champion of the World, so it was most unlikely David was going to beat me, then came the game of pool, it was rare he would beat me in that either, then came darts, now there's no way I could touch him in that, he was brilliant, after beating me at darts the aggression that had built up over the last few contests (and they were contests) slowly subsided, over the years David has slowly mellowed and become a very likable lad, there had been times when I could easily have said get lost son and meant it, you cant always blame everything on your childhood, but it can take only one woman, to spoil a young person life.

David has a younger half Brother James, they get along like an house on fire, considering they weren't brought up together, James stayed at home even though his father left his Mother, while David was shunted around into different homes, I have read all David's Social workers reports from the time he went into care until the time he left, and all the problems he had pointed to one person, if only I had known the future of my son at that early age, the time I saw him in a home when he was three, I was told he was only there because he had severe Asthma, and he would be coming home shortly, she lied, I lost fifteen years of watching my son grow up and turning into a young man, with all the worries he had to endure in his adolescent years, David and James are still very close to this day, and although David calls me Dad, we're like best buddies, and maybe I don't tell him this often enough, but I love him and I'm very proud of him.

THE BLETCHLEY ARM'S

The Arms was a much bigger pub than the Bow Bell, and the wages were a lot more so in I moved. After a few days we noticed a funny smell and over the following weeks it got stronger, so I phoned the new area manager that had taken over from Mr Hankestone and told him about this smell. "Lift the carpet lift the floorboards you might find a dead rat," he said, 'I don't think so, if I lift the carpet, I will never be able to lay it again' I said. So nothing was done about it, and the smell stayed. People were now walking in the front door and moving straight to the other end of the bar. It was a Saturday morning when I called beer services out, because on the Friday night I had changed a twenty two-gallon barrel of Holsten and Saturday lunchtime it was empty. We were busy but not that busy to empty a twenty two-gallon barrel. An old boy called George came down from beer services to sort it out, he went in the cellar to pressure test the pipes, when he had finished he told me all the pipes were ok. The following day I had a stock-take, it was Roy the same stock-taker that I had at the Bow Bell, even he mentioned about the smell and I told him what the area manager had said, and he even said it wasn't my job to be lifting carpets.

A few hours later Roy had finished the stock and said he would phone me a couple of days later with the result. I thanked him and he left.

Three days later he was back, apologising that he had to do a walk in stock. 'What does that mean?' I asked. "It means you had a bad stock and I have to do another now," 'fine' I said. 'I have nothing to hide Roy.' He said, "he knows that but it really was a bad deficit," 'how much?' I asked. Four thousand was his reply. 'How much?.' I screamed. Do that fucking stock again and you're not leaving here until I have the results. In the mean time I had phoned beer service again for another check on my lines. The guy had just arrived when my area manager showed his face. Blimey John what's that awful smell? That's the smell I told you about three weeks ago, and you did nothing about it. He used his phone then took me over to a corner table for a chat.

"Have you got any financial problems?" he asked. 'I beg your pardon' was my reply. I couldn't believe what I was hearing, but he said it again. "Have you got any financial problems?" I lent across the table nice and slowly and said, 'if you say that again there's a window behind you, and you will be going straight through it, I haven't just thrown in my career to come into this game where I get paid a lot less wages than I did when I was wrestling, to rip the fucking brewery off. "No! No I can understand that, but I had to ask you because my boss is going to ask me if I asked you that."

'Well there's a way of asking those kind of questions, and that my friend, was definitely the wrong fucking way.' With that, he got up and left.

Soon after, a guy arrived that I knew from beer services. "Hello John, I heard on the van radio that you had a problem here." 'Yes I have, but George is here trying to sort it out.' "Well two heads are better than one as the saying goes" he said and off he went to the cellar. I followed just to see what or if there was anything I could do. "What you doing George?" asked the second guy. "Pressurising the lines," he said. "Not with that poundage" said the second guy. As he knocked the poundage up from fifteen to thirty, the needle shot up to the top of the dial and then started coming down again. "There's your proble," said George, "you have a hole in your pipe on the Carlsberg." It wasn't Carlsberg I was worried about it was the Holsten. "We'll try the lot and come back to you." It was about twenty minuets later when George came to me and said, "you have four lines with holes in, what we'll have to do is take the boards up from behind the bar to get to the clay pipe that holds all the lines in place." As they proceeded to roll back the lino and lift the boards I made a phone call to my area manager to let him know we had found the problem. He informed me that there was a letter on the way to me and I should disregard it. Roy the stock-taker made an appearance, not knowing what the fuck was going on. He had a sullen look on his face. "I'm sorry John but in three days your just under five hundred pounds down in stock. I can't say what's going to happen, but I think the least you are looking at is a disciplinary." Just then we heard a shout, "fucking hell, look at this lot." As we walked behind the bar a swarm of yeast flies came out from under the boards that had been lifted. Christ almighty there's a lake down here. I was called over to take a look, the smell was terrible. "How long had these lines been leaking, because this mess goes all the way back to the toilets George said,." 'You tell me George I asked, because a few weeks ago when I called you out you said there was nothing wrong with the pipes," I've never seen a mans face colour up so quick. "You reported this before?" Roy said. 'You know I have Roy, I even told you what the area manager told me to do, this could have been sorted weeks a go if somebody had taken the time to investigate it properly, I've only been in this game a short while, and never encountered anything like it, but the disgusting smell and the loss of beer told me something was wrong, but nobody listened.' Roy was in a raging mood, right he said I will get all this written off, and I will make sure none of this comes back on you John. I thanked him and he left, I'm sure I saw steam coming from his ears as he went through the door. I never opened that afternoon, as they had to put new lines in. When they showed me the old lines they had taken out they told me I had rats. The lines had been chewed through, not pinholes, bloody great holes; it's no wonder that I lost so much stock. The following day the letter arrived from the area manager. It stated that I should take this letter as a final warning, that I was incompetent, and if ever I had a bad stock again I would be dismissed. The arsehole never had the guts to tell me to my face, in fact he never came near me for at least three months, and I never received an apology either. We spoke on the phone and he couldn't have been nicer, but he knew he was a two faced shit-house rat, and so did I.

It was mid January on a Tuesday night, and Jean was doing the cleaning after we had closed, as we never had a cleaner on a Wednesday morning. I had just finished counting the tills and doing the paper work and was about to sit down with a cup of coffee when I heard the scream. Did it come from out side, or was it Jean? I thought. Then it happened again and it was Jean. I was sitting there just with my pants on, but I legged it down stairs as fast as my legs would go. As I came into the bar Jean was at the end of the counter, outside the bar with the hatch closed. "It's there?" she said, screeching and panicking. 'What's there?' I said. "A rat" she said. 'Don't be daft' I said, and as I moved the canister from under the bar, I saw a bit of a tail, it's a bloody mouse I thought to myself, I moved the canister a bit more and I saw more of the tail, now I'm thinking to myself, this mouse has a bloody long tail when all of a sudden the bloody thing made a run for it. Jean legged it out into the garden and I legged it up stairs. I was only wearing my pants for Christ sake. On went my trousers and shoes and my zip up jacket. I grabbed my high-powered slug gun and ran down the stairs again but this time I took the dogs. A fucking lot of good they were, they took one sniff then pissed off up stairs again. That rat was waiting for me I'm sure, because as I entered the kitchen there it was sitting in the middle of the room up on it's hunches, then it made a dart behind the up right fridge freezer, but when I looked it wasn't there. I went all round that bloody room tapping on this tapping on that and it wasn't until I got to the chest freezer that I saw it. I moved the freezer to one side so it couldn't get out, I didn't want to look at it again so I put the gun round the corner and let about seven ball bearings go, I said it was a high powered repeating pistol, well it made a bit of a mess of that rat. To give you some idea of the size of it, when I picked it up on a standard dustpan, lengthwise it was hanging over the ends.

From that time on Jean wanted out of there, she said if we've got rats in the bar there's every chance that there up stairs as well, and I'm not sharing my place with them. We found they were coming from the cinema next door that had been closed for three years.

A week or two after moving into the Bletchley Arms a couple came to see me and said they had been offered the Bow Bell, and was told to come and see me to get the low down on the place. I didn't hold anything back, I told them exactly how it was. I told them all the shit they could expect to get, but after speaking with Roger and Doreen for a good half hour, I told them they could make a go of it, they had the right temperament for the place. He wasn't a big hard man but I could tell he wouldn't stand for any shit, and he had this cheeky smile, not that he was a young guy because he wasn't but he acted a lot younger than his years, and I could see him mucking in with the lads, playing pool and generally being friendly, that's what they wanted, not someone who would lay down the law and stick to the letter of it. If they went in laying the law down they would definitely get a hard time.

As it was I was right, Roger made a great governor, and we became very good friends. We arranged pool and dart competitions between the two pubs, we even had a drinking competition once.

One day I asked Roger if he would like to come training with me at the leisure centre,

I wouldn't mind "but don't you go trying to cripple me" he said. 'Of course I wouldn't' said I. I wrote out a little program for him to do. "That's easy enough, just three sets of three" he said. 'Yes, but between each set you have to do ten free squats, will that be all right? I asked. "Show me what you mean and I'll see if I can do them" he said, so I showed him. I stood with my feet apart and bent my knees until my arse was about six inches from the ground, 'now you try' I said. He did it without any problems. "Easy peesy" he said. I started him off with lightweights and all he had to do was three repartitions of pull downs behind the neck. When he had finished that he had to do ten free squats, then another three pull downs, and another ten squats, by the time he had finished doing all the pull downs, then the bench presses, and then the sit ups, he had actually done ninety squats. 'That wasn't hard was it,' I asked. I thought you was going to take the piss and put me through the pain barrier," he said. 'No, not me, I wouldn't dream of it,' I said.

The following morning I got the phone call. "You dirty rotten black bastard, I can't move my fucking legs you twat, what have you done to me? I cant even get out of the fucking bed," When I eventually stopped laughing I told him to take a shower and rub the backs of his legs hard, then do as many squats as he can too stretch the muscles and he would be alright after that. Every time I see Roger now, that afternoon is always mentioned.

I let my area manager and the head office know that we wanted out of the Bletchley Arms, because until they did something with the cinema next door we were still being over run with rats. It took about two months before I had a call from an area manager from Dunstable asking if I was still interested in moving. I assured him I was and he offered me a pub called the Sportsman in Katherine Drive Dunstable. I thanked him and told him I would get back to him after speaking to the wife. That night I went to see my old buddy Roger at the Bow bells. I asked him if he knew the pub, and would he like it. I knew he would say yes because he had his house not half a mile away from it. I got back in touch with the area manager and explained that Roger was very interested in moving to Dunstable, and he knows the pub very well and knows what it's like. "So your not interested in moving John" he said. 'Yes' I said, when Roger moves to Dunstable I can have the Bow Bell back, and that's exactly what happened. I went back to the Bow Bell, and stayed for two and a half years, and my friend Roger fell in love with his new pub.

THE FIRST TRIP TO HAMBURG

My pub wasn't completely trouble free for the two and a half years I was there.

But we had more good times than we had bad. I was there for three months before I arranged the first trip of many abroad. The first trip saw us off for a long weekend to Hamburg, Germany. There were nine of us and we flew out from Stanstead airport. On arriving in Hamburg we took a taxi to the Reeperbhan and the Hotel Wellar. I had already phoned my friend Klaus about six weeks prior to reserve the hotel rooms, it's where I used to stay when I was wrestling in Hamburg, and it's the old! Old! Saying, it's not what you know, it's who you know that counts, and he had given me a bloody good discount on the rooms. The bar underneath the hotel was also his. Now don't get carried away but the name of the bar was called (Sex and Drisic) which in German means thirty-six. I have known Klaus and his wife Helgar for at least thirty-six years and a nicer couple you couldn't wish to meet, they have only recently sold their Hotel and bar, and retired for a well-earned rest. The Hotel is still called Wellar's but the Bar is now called P.J's. In the reception of the hotel they still have some photos of the wrestlers hanging there, and I'm proud to say my photo is still amongst them.

On arrival back at the pub they all said they really enjoyed themselves and when was the next trip. I thought they were joking but at least once a week some one would ask if I was arranging another trip, I was once told keep the punters happy and they will keep coming back.

So another trip was arranged, this time to Hamburg Beer Fest at the beginning of November, but this time we would be travelling by ship from Harwich straight into Hamburg, this meant that they would only have about half a day actually in Hamburg. The itinerary was, a coach would pick us up from the pub and take us to Harwich where we would board the ship to Hamburg. We sailed about four p.m in the after-noon. We all had cabins, some had four people sharing and some had two sharing. After ditching our bag we all met in the main bar at the front of the ship. I gave a short speech on how to conduct ones self when they land in Germany, and if any one finds they have a problem come and find me. Don't get into a fight, because you will be locked up straight away and will miss the ship home, then that becomes your problem, not mine. There was some great entertainment on board that night as well as a casino, where I lost a few bob. I think most of the boys were well pissed by the time they went to bed because they didn't look to clever at breakfast time. The ship docked around eight thirty. It was a cold and windy morning.

By the time we got through customs the coach was waiting to take us too town, or the Reeperbhan, most of the lad's had heard so much about the Reeperbhan that the town was a no, no.

I asked the coach driver to stop just the other side of the traffic lights, which he did, right outside the Wellar Hotel. My friend Klaus was behind his bar, when he saw all these people getting off the coach he nearly had a heart attack. There was my crew and a lot of people that my lot had made friends with the previous night. When Klaus recognized me a big grin came across his face. "Johnny my friend, I have not got enough beds," I quickly explained that we were not stopping over night, that we came by ship, but I had to show my friends your bar. With my crew and about fifteen other people Klaus was a very busy boy for the next hour or so, the good thing was I never had to by a beer the whole time I was there. Before the lads started to leave the bar I told them all that the ship sailed again at five p.m so make sure they are back on board by four thirty, and if their not they would have to find there own way home, and that could be very expensive.

I said my good byes to Klaus and told him I would see him around March or April the following year, 'but next time I would need some rooms.' "No problem, and I will give you the best price" he said. Klaus looked after me and my boys for twenty odd years, and I still get a Christmas card from him.

THE BAD TIMES

Like the time I kept a few back for a late drink. Everything was going well, plenty of laughing and joking going on and I was playing pool with this guy called Ray. After a while Ray asked if he could have another drink. 'Sure mate' I said. As I went behind the bar Ray came to the counter and the expression on his face changed, he was kind of looking over my shoulder to the left, so I followed his glance, he was looking at the mirror behind the bar and he could see his wife snogging a guy behind the pillar at the end of the bar. I asked him if he wanted another game or did he want to go home? "I think another game's in order, your two frames up on me so far he said. As he was talking his wife came and sat beside him. "Show me your chest Mr wrestler," she said. "Shut up slag" said Ray. "I'm talking to a man not a mouse," said she. With that he swung his arm around and knocked her clean off her seat. I shouted at him to stop right there because it looked to me that he wanted to keep on bashing her. Not in my place I shouted, I don't give a shit what you do at home, but you don't do it in here. "You can shut up or I'll blow your fucking legs of," he said. I remember walking from behind the bar and seeing Ray shape up to me! (Putting his fists up). That's all I remember, until I became aware of Jean standing in front of me telling me to put it down. Put what down I was thinking to myself, then I became aware of the stool I was holding above my head. We were now at the other end of the bar (the London end) and all the guys were standing around with their backs to the wall as if to give me space, and there laid Ray flat out on his back. His wife was sitting on a step leading to the eyelevel-screaming kill him John, kill him! 'Someone shut her up for fucks sake' I said, as I put down the stool and picked up Ray. I laid him down on the bench seat next to the fruit machine, Jean brought a glass of brandy over and said, "sit him up and give him this, and then send them both home, we don't want any more trouble do we, do you understand me?" she asked looking into my eyes. I nodded, and then asked her what had happened. "You blacked out, and if you hadn't come back when you did you would have caved in his skull with that stool." I drank the brandy, and asked her to fetch another one for him. As Ray came round I said 'drink this my old son and you'll feel better,' he downed it in one. I got him to his feet and walked him to the door, I pointed to his wife and said to her, 'take him home now, and I mean now, no backchat! Just take him home.' I opened the door and they left like an old married couple, his arm around her shoulder and her arm around his waist, a few months later Ray was stabbed to death, apparently for saying the wrong thing again.

I prided myself on never rushing my punters out of the pub at closing time. After the last bell had gone I would go around asking people to drink up, but I wouldn't demand their glasses there and then, and it worked, maybe it took them half an hour, but they left happy and with a smile on their faces, but you always get the odd one who would try and take the piss, and get smart, or try and back chat you,

When you have spent all day pulling pints and listening to drunks you can really do without some smart arse trying to be clever at closing time, and I must admit after eleven thirty at night I'm on a short fuse.

There were two large tables put together up on the eye-level and about ten or twelve Geordies (guys from Newcastle) sitting around them. I had spoken to a few of them throughout the night and they seemed decent lads. The last bell had sounded and I was making my rounds, when I got to their table I said in a friendly voice, lets have your glasses please lads and I was turning away when one of the crowd said, "yeh, you'll get them when we're finished." Now that's got my back up straight away,

They're dictating to me in my own pub, I don't think so. I walked back to the table and said 'your all finished now' and I went to pick a glass up and this stupid man grabbed it as well. I said, 'I'm taking this glass and if any of this beer goes over me you will be hitting the deck.' With that two guys on the other side of the table stood up, I let go of the glass and said 'more my age more my size' and I started to walk around the table, They sat back down as fast as they got up, then I noticed why, all the boys from the London end and all the boys from the Scots end had congregated in the middle of the bar and looking towards the table, I said. 'I think its best you drink up now and leave with out saying another word, and I will guarantee no one will get hurt, but it will only take one of you to say something smart and I wont be responsible for the out come.' It was the quietest I have ever heard anybody leave a pub, if only the smart arse that opened his mouth in the first place had kept it shut, they could have sat there and maybe had afters (a late drink) all night.

Another little incident I remember concerned two brothers. I had just returned home from a wrestling match in Aylesbury. The time must have been around eleven thirty or quarter to twelve. Jean wasn't in a very good mood. I enquired what was wrong as she took my arm and led me to the foyer. "Have a look at that" she said. The bottom half of the window panel was missing. 'What the fuck happened there?' I asked. Then she proceeded to tell me that the two brothers went out side to have a fight, when it was all over one of them kicked the window in, then came in and asked for a drink. Jean told him there was no way he was going to get a drink and it would be appreciated if he picked the glass up that he put his foot through, with that he let lose with a torrent of abusive language, and when my step daughter Mandy stepped forward to try and calm the situation down, she got it as well. It was a couple of the Scottish lads that bundled him out the door, they had their wives with them and they didn't want to hear that kind language with them around.

One of them asked Jean, "Does that idiot know who your old man is? She said, she didn't know, but she was sure he would find out soon enough, which he did the following day. The following morning I managed to find out the address of the brothers, so I jumped in my car and drove round there. As I pulled up out side their place one of the brothers pulled up in front of me. "Hello John, if it's about last night." 'Where's your brother?' I asked. "In the house" came the reply with a look of relief on his face that I never came after him. His brother opened the door; he took about four steps back before falling on his arse. As I stepped over the thresh-hold his father came out of his front room and said he'll call the police. I said, 'and you have every right to, because I have stepped over your thresh-hold, but I wouldn't dream of coming into your house and calling your wife a slag, a Blackman lover and a whore, and then calling the same things to your daughter.' By this time the brother had picked himself up and peered over his dad's shoulder, when a fist hit him smack bang in the middle of the forehead. 'Now you can call the police' I said as I turned and walked out. The police were never called. The following day Alex came to the pub, he sincerely apologised to Jean and said it was all done in the heat of the moment, (we have all been there) and it will never happen again, the apology was accepted.

The captain of the pool team who's name is Pat came to me one day and said that his house had been broken into the previous night and they had taken a few things including his V.H.S recorder, and if I hear anything would I let him know. Naturally I said I would. A few days had passed when a name came back to me, and the guy in question came waltzing into the pub. It was nice and quiet at the time so I thought I would have a word with him. 'I understand you have Pat's video' I said. "No I haven't" said he. 'Let's put it this way then, you had Pat's video.' "It didn't work so I got rid of it" he said. 'It didn't matter if it worked or not he had a video he could have got repaired, so now he would like it replaced,' I said. "I can get him one but it will cost him", he said. 'Fuck off, you nicked it in the first place I said, you either get him a video or leave,' meaning leave the estate, as he was only bumming around living with so called friends on the estate. "No", he said. 'What does no mean?' I asked. "Neither" he said. With that he put his face right up to mine and said, "neither means I wont get him a fucking video and I wont be leaving the estate either." He should never have put his face that close to mine, because when he spoke he sprayed and to me there is nothing worse than spit hitting your face, when my forehead connected with his nose I knew it was broken, it was a sound I had heard many times over the years, I pushed him back into the lobby, and as my hand was on his face he tried to bite my thumb, but I managed to hook it inside his mouth and I ripped his mouth from back to front, I lost my temper and after whacking him a few more times I told him to go home and get his knife and come back. (He was known for using a blade). I told him I would take his knife off of him and cut his arse to pieces so every time he went to sit down he wouldn't forget me, with that I pushed him out the door. My shirt was covered in blood, there was nobody at this time in the pub, the three that were there probably heard the commotion and decided to piss off. I closed the doors and went up stairs to change. Jean was out shopping so I put the shirt in the basin with salt water, I desperately needed to get out of the pub to calm down, so I took a slow ride around town and pulled into the Bletchley Arms for a cup of coffee and a chat with the new governor. When I eventually got back to the pub Jean was home and going frantic, she had seen the shirt in the sink and thought something terrible had happened to me, I assured her I was all right and the blood wasn't mine.

Later that night the person in question came back into the bar. I was slightly tooled up as I expected some kind of retaliation; he came up to me and asked though very swollen lips if he was barred. I said for having so much front mate, no, but Pat still wants his V.H.S. back. I'm sure it was more in defiance than anything else that he stayed all night drinking through a straw.

It wasn't until the first bell had gone when the bottle hit the window. I rushed out to see this Scottish person legging it towards the London Pride pub. I took chase but as he approached the steps leading down to the pub he started to slow down when in fact he could have jumped them with the speed he was going. Beside the steps was a wall with some very high bushes, now maybe it was the game I was in before that made me aware, alert, cautious of what was happening around me. I took out the starting pistol as I got to the top of the stairs and fired it in to the bushes. There were shouts of he's got a gun! As three or four lads legged it along the walkway throwing down the various sticks and pool cues as they went. I returned to my pub. The man with the fat lips had gone, a few of my customers said I was mad going out there by myself, anything could have happened. I told them I am here to protect my customers and if that bottle had come through the window some one could have been seriously hurt. It wasn't more than fifteen minuets later when the police came in. "Hello John the sergeant said, we've just heard over the radio that someone from these premises chased somebody with a hand pistol, i.e you." 'Yes' I said. "Did you really John," he asked. 'Look at me I said, I'm Roy Rogers and I always carry two guns. Who was it that called you, was it a Scottish lad? because if it was you could run up behind him clap your hands hard, and he would shit himself.' "So you never left these premises all night?" he asked. 'I never said that sergeant, I chased the little twat, yes, because he threw a bottle at my window and if I had caught the little fucker there's no doubt you would be locking me up, but as for using a hand pistol, that's a load of crap.' A day or two later the sergeant came back in to see me, and asked if I would like a gun licence, (my skin colour is brown, not green) 'what do I want a gun licence for? I enquired, I don't get time for a pony let alone get time to go shooting.' "Well, anytime you acquire a gun you come and see me and I will sign the forms for you" he said. I thanked him, and assured him I would never be coming to him for a gun licence, my inner senses told me not to trust him, and I always go with my feeling.

It was the following week when Pat came to me and said "thank you." 'What's the thank you for? I enquired.' "Somebody left a video recorder on the door-step yesterday and I have a funny feeling you had something to do with it." I gave him a knowing smile and said, "a word in the right ear sometimes does the trick, and we will leave it at that.' Pat pulled out all the stops that pool season, and we won the pool league for the very first time.

The worst thing that ever happened in the pub was one Christmas Eve. After we closed I sat down with two of my bar maids for a social Christmas drink before they went home. After they left I locked up and went up stairs to help Jean. It couldn't have been more than ten minutes when I got the phone call, it was Elaine one of the bar maids, she was crying her heart out, some dirty rotten shithouse rat had broken into her house and stole all her kids Christmas presents. Her kids were staying with a neighbour until she got home, so it must have been someone who saw that she was working and knew that the house would be empty, because she never left the kids alone, now that is the lowest of the low. After a week or so a name came up but it could never be proved. A funny thing happened to me years later and the same name was involved, but that's another story.

One of the best area managers I ever had was a guy called Danny Hobden. He came to me one day and asked if I knew of anybody who could run a pub. I may do I said, why? He told me he needed someone to run the Bletchley Arms until they close it down for a refurbishment in about three to four months time. I told him I thought I knew of a couple that might be able to do it, I would ask them and get back to him,

Pat and Patsy, the guy who ran my pool team and his wife have longed to run a pub for some time, and they jumped at the chance as soon as I mentioned it. They didn't know the first thing about running a pub, but I told them if it was alright with my area manager I would come down every day and teach them the paper work and computer work as well as the cellar and beer ordering. The first thing Danny asked me was, can I trust them because it would be on my head if anything went wrong. With my life I said, he agreed to meet them and give them the once over. Patsy had been a bar maid in various pubs so she knew how to pull a pint but Pat god bless him gave more head (as in pint) than beer. I was there every day for about seven weeks, then I let them have the reigns, and said, 'only phone me if you really get stuck.' I must have made a good job of training them as I only got one phone call in the time they had left.

Pat and Patsy knew that when the Bletchley Arms closed for the refurbishment they would have to leave the pub, but I did tell them that I would try and get them on to the company through the back door. I kept on to my area manager that they did a bloody good job for a couple that had never run a pub before. Pat and Patsy had about two weeks at home before they were offered a pub in Leighton Buzzard (The Market Tavern) which they ran for a couple of years.

Danny came to see me with a proposition. He said that the big men in the office came up with an idea for a new name at the Bletchley Arms; they want to call it Kincaid's, and they want you to run it, what do you think of that? 'Very nice I said, and I suppose you want my name for nothing?' Remember I was still wrestling at this time and appearing regularly on T.V, so the company would be guaranteed free advertisement, so I didn't think a few shilling for the use of my name would be to much to ask fore. Danny said they expected to pay something, but it depended on how much I wanted. Well to cut a long story short, I couldn't have asked for enough because they didn't even try to knock me down, Bollocks I thought, well some you

win and some you lose, that's the way the cookie crumbles.

The refurbishment had just started on the Bletchley Arms when I took my family on holiday. I had a competent relief manager in the Bow Bell looking after things so I had no worries there, how wrong can one be. On my early morning arrival back in the country I was about to tuck up in my bed at home when I noticed a note on the side table from my daughter, which said! Site meeting brought forward to ten thirty. The time was around five o'clock a .m, was it worth going to sleep I asked my self. I snatched a couple of hours sleep, showered, and then made my way to the Bletchley Arms. There was about eight of us sitting at this long bench table when one of the workmen shouted out "Johnny your wanted on the phone." I made my way over to the ladder that substituted for the stairs as they were repositioning the stairs to another part of the landing. On reaching the phone I said, 'hello.' "They've nicked the safe" came the reply. 'Who is this?' I asked. "It's Peter, your relief manager at the Bow Bell." 'So what do you mean they've nicked the safe, you mean the money don't you?' "No, the fucking safe" he said.

I know I shouldn't have, but I just started laughing my head off, and in between my hysterical laughter I told him not to worry and I will get back to him. I took a minute or two to control myself before descending the ladder, and taking my place back at the table, I tried to keep a straight face, a sullen face, and when my area manager looked at me he said, "what's wrong John you look like you have the troubles of the world on your shoulders? 'Not me' I said, you, that was the Bow Bell on the phone and the manager has just informed me that someone has nicked the safe.' "Don't you mean the money John? 'No the fucking safe' I said. "Oh shit" he said as he tried to hop over the bench seat we were all sitting on, falling and nearly knocking himself out. I couldn't keep it in any longer, I doubled over with laughter. Sorry I said to Danny, just when I thought nothing else could go wrong today, you go and nose-dive the floor. At the time he didn't see the funny side of things, but thank god he had a sense of humour and saw the funny side of things when I explained to him the happenings of the day so far.

The following day I stocked back into the Bow Bell, needless to say my stock was going to be down which is a usual thing with agency relief workers but I thought I had compensated for that before I left for my holidays,

I hadn't counted on the loss of the weekend takings as well. It transpires that the relief manager took a lady friend to a night club and stayed out all night, so there was nobody on site, and he had left my dogs up stairs, not roaming the bar area or cellar. We never had a spare room either so

He had to use our bedroom that was the first and last time that ever happened. It came back to me a bit later (you know how customers talk) that he had two or three ladies up stairs, shagging them in my bed; he also pissed the bed, which cost me a new mattress. He, or one of his lady friends burnt a hole in the arm of my new three-piece suite, and there was a burn hole in the carpet, so who had the last fucking laugh, it certainly wasn't me.

It must have been a month later when I found out who had the safe away. A few nights later when this particular person came in I sidled up to him and whispered in his ear, 'where's my safe mate? He spluttered in his beer. 'Don't deny it, I know it was you' I said. He started to laugh and that cheeky grin spread right across his face. "Look John, I never touched any of your stuff, I didn't touch your desk and I didn't go up stairs." 'Just as well, the dogs would have chewed your bollocks off' I said. "Are they that bad?" he asked. 'Ask any of my bar maids, they have all had there arse bitten at one time or another,' and then he started to laugh again. "Can I tell you what happened John?" he asked. "Be my guest" said I well we were standing at the bar having a beer minding our own business, when we heard the boss asking this girl out for a drink, we heard one of them mention Razelles night club so we knew that it would be a late night for them, we left the pub at closing time and came back at twelve thirty, the back gate to the yard was open so we drove the van up to the back door, after getting the door open it took us less than four minutes to get the safe in the back of the van, then we were gone. We left the safe in the van, in the garage for a couple of days, then we drove over to the Blue Lagoon where we were going to burn the door off, but as we rolled the safe out of the van the handle of the safe hit the bumper, and before the safe hit the ground the bloody door flew open, after all we went through the fucking thing wasn't even locked."

'Now you can do me a favour' I said. "Fuck off John you don't want the safe back?" he said. 'No, but you can bring back my fucking sack barrow, I'm fed up carrying crates out to the bar by hand.' The barrow was returned the very next day.

PAULA, FIT FINLAY, AND THE BOY'S

One evening I had a phone call from Paula Finnlay the wife of Dave Fit Finlay,

She said that Dave, Skull Murphy, Drew McDonald, had been wrestling in Croydon London and would it be alright if they called in on the way home to Manchester, the only thing is they wouldn't get to my place until after closing, I said, after closing is my social time and they would be welcome any time, I let a few of my regulars stay behind for a late drink, but I never told them who was coming. Later when there was a tap on the door I shouted to my mate Eric to open the door for me. Now my mate Eric is not a big lad in stature, and I don't think he would mind me saying he looked quite puny against the three lads that had just walked in. The rest of the lads couldn't take there eyes of Paula with her long black hair hanging down to her back side, and her full figure hugging dress. I asked Dave if we could have a bit of a laugh with Paula, he said he was game if she was. I took Paula over to meet a few of my friends. This is Ginger

John I said, and this one is Ron the Bread, this is Tom the Painter, and this is Eric. As Eric put his hand out to shake, Paula took him straight up on to her shoulders and started to aeroplane spin him. I had visions of everyone getting sprayed because El had a gut full of beer. She only spun him about five times and as she put him down he went all over the place, out came his infectious laugh, "I thought I was going to shit myself" he said. 'And we all thought you were going to puke' I replied.

Paula is no relation of mine, but I have called her my sister for a number of years,

It all started at a wrestling show in Newbury. Paula had been wrestling this night and afterwards had gone to the bar for a drink. I saw her talking to a guy at the end of the bar so I kept my distance. After a while the guy turned and looked at me, turned back to Paula then took a double take at me, a few more words were spoken then he left, Paula had this almighty great grin on her face as she beckoned me over. "Thanks brother" she said. I must have had this funny look on my face because she went on to explain that the guy who was talking to her was telling her that he could show her some good holds that she would really like, she told him she was sure he could and that she wouldn't mind but she didn't think her brother would like it much if she went out side with him. "Who's your brother?" he asked, and she said he's standing at the other end of the bar, that's when he turned and saw me. "That's Johnny Kincaid" he said. "That's right" she said, "he's my brother and I bet he comes over within the next two minutes she said, "shit he said, please don't tell him what we were talking about he will kill me," and made a quick exit. Ever since then Princess Paula has been my sister.

THE KINCAID'S

It was the month of March when the Bletchley Arms refurb was finished. From the outside it still looked like a pub, but the inside had totally changed, it looked like a top class nightclub. As you entered the front porch you were looking up the full length of the pub which was about one hundred and twenty five yards long, and as you left the porch and entered the pub there was a mirrored ceiling above you with pin spot lights all around it, the bar it self was painted with a green front and beige top, the back bar was a fawn colour with green neon lights, at the other end of the bar there was a dance floor and a disco booth, above the dance floor was twenty three grand's worth of disco lighting and two mirror balls, the lighting was in sync with the D.J booths music, the big a-la-carte kitchen that we used to have had now been turned into a bloody great recess with bench seating and tables around it, it also had three big beautiful animal print pictures, the lighting consisted of spot lights and ceiling pin spots, all columns were mirrored as were parts of walls, so in affect you would call it a posers pub. We were due

Johnny Kincaid

to open at six thirty that evening, the carpet was still being laid at two o'clock, and the pool table couldn't be brought in until the carpet was laid.

The toilets looked lovely, white tiles in the gents, they had taken the trough away and put in single urinals with silver ashtrays between each one, and a colourful durex machine by the door, the ladies were done out in pink tiles with pink hand basins, it also had a durex machine in it, plus a tampon machine.

I had two area managers behind the bar putting up optics, while Jean and I were filling up the shelves with bottles. It was all finished and ready to open at a quarter to six, so we all sat down for a nice cup of tea. It had taken six weeks to transform the old Bletchley Arms into the new Kincaid's, it was never officially called Kincaid's only Kincaid because some bright spark in the office said if somebody knocks out the first four letters of my name it would leave (Aids), they actually pay people to think of things like that, but what he or she never thought of was, if somebody broke one letter on a neon light they would all go out because they were joined, but the long and the short of it was, people still called it Kincaid's.

I remember the first person coming through the door as if it was yesterday, he stood in the door way admiring the place, then he came over to me and ordered a drink, and said "it looks great Johnny, have you got a pool table?" I told him it was around the corner. "Fancy a game" he asked. 'While its quite I'll give you a game' I said. I passed him fifty pence and told him to set the balls up and I'll bring his beer round to him, I had poured his beer and was taking it around to him when I noticed him drop a lighted cigarette on the floor and put his foot on it, I said to him 'what's that under your foot? He looked bemused and said "a fag butt." I said, 'pick it up and fuck off.' "You are joking of cause" he said. 'Stand there for another five seconds and you will be joining your fag butt on the floor, this carpet hasn't been down four hours yet and there's new ashtrays everywhere you look and you had to put your fag out on my new carpet.' I think he could tell I wasn't pissing about so he picked it up a bit smartish and left the building. To say I was a little vexed would be an understatement; I played the game of pool by myself and drank his beer. This was a Friday night and it was around seven o'clock before the first batch of customers arrived. I was starting to get worried because the place had been closed for six weeks and the old customers might have got settled into other pubs and wanted to stay there, but slowly the place started to fill up, the lights were dimmed and the colourful lights over the dance floor were jumping to the music, I had three staff on duty plus myself and Jean, and we were working our butts off. This one guy kept shouting out to me, John, John! I said 'I will be with you in a moment.' John, John! I thought fuck him, he can wait now so I served another four or five customers then went to him. 'What do you want I asked? He pointed behind me at the open door that led to the cellar, at the end of the corridor stood my ice machine, a pipe had come off and water was pissing out all over the place. 'Why didn't you say something?' I said. "I called but you didn't take any notice" he said.

Johnny Kincaid

Some people haven't got the brains they were born with, he could have said John you've got a leak.

I couldn't believe how the place was taking off, Saturday lunchtime the place was heaving, people I had never seen before coming in and asking for the Big Daddy cocktail and the Kincaid Specials and the Haystack Splash, they were inquiring what music we had on, on any given night. We put music on every night except Tuesdays, as it was my night off, and it was also pool night. Every night we had different kinds of music, from barn dancing, (coach loads of American servicemen from Chicksands American base came down) Rock and Roll, Jazz, Soul and Reggae, and pure dance music, and once a week we had a live band. Kincaid's took of with a bang, we had our teething problems but Kincaid's was the place to be.

BOMBER PAT ROACH

Bomber Pat Roach did me the honour of opening the pub for me, and he pulled in a bloody big crowd.

The week before hand I was booked to wrestle in a T.V contest in Hemel Hampstead, On arrival the promoter pulled me to one side, and asked me if it would be alright if he took me out of the single match I was booked for, and put me in a four man knockout tournament, because one of the contestants in the four man had broken his ankle the night previous, and as it was a heavyweight tournament, he could put me in and put a lower weight in my match, and make it a catch-weight contest, so I agreed. Just as I approached the dressing room door it opened and big Pat was standing there, "you're a week early John" he said and we both laughed. We were sitting there talking when Brian Dixon the promoter came in with a beer mug, he offered each of us the mug to take a piece of paper which had a number on, I had number two, Ray Steel had number four, Pat had number one and Dalibar Singh number three, so me and Pat were drawn together, I said to him 'look here you big bastard, if you hurt me, your not going to earn any money down my place next week. It was a fifteen minute contest, I managed to get a fall in or around the twelfth minute, but the big man knocked me out around the fourteenth minute, gentle giant Ha, he wasn't gentle with me that night but he was still one of my best mates in the wrestling game.

It took a week before all the ashtrays in the toilets disappeared, not that whoever stole them was going to use them at home or even sell them because they were worth nothing.

A friend of mine worked on Chilton Radio as a D.J playing Soul and Reggie, so I asked him if he could work a Wednesday night for me for a couple of weeks just to see how it would go. He gave me and the pub a bit of publicity and told his listeners that he would be down Kincaid's on Wednesday night playing some of their favourite tunes and he would like to see some of them there. They came from everywhere, Dunstable, Luton, Northampton, Bedford, to name a few places. That first Wednesday was something else, I couldn't get another person in if I tried, there were people standing out side the front of the building dancing. My back garden was full of people dancing, and I had seven bar staff working, what a night. It wasn't until we closed and I was going round locking up that I found some clever twat had pulled the down pipe off one of the urinals and had flooded the toilet, I found the stop-cock and switched it off, the following morning I had to phone for a plumber, I would like to say that this was just a one off thing but every Wednesday the same thing happened, eventually

I never had to phone for the plumber he automatically came the next day. I eventually found out it was one of my own regulars that was doing it, because he didn't like out of Towner's coming into his pub, I had to put him straight on this matter, that this wasn't his pub, it was mine, and I was there to make as much money as I could, and I didn't want to spend out each week on repairs, and if it happened again I would be all over him like a rash and he wouldn't like it, I should have barred him or got him to pay back some of the money I had spent out on repairs, but I did neither, and it turned out to be the right thing to do, he became my doorman and a very good friend.

Being a Disco pub it attracted a lot of young people and some of them were under age. One night I was sitting upstairs when my daughter Tasha came out with a remark about some of her school friends liking the pub. I said, 'your school friends shouldn't be in the pub,' she then realized what she had said and tried to get out of it by saying they only saw it when they came calling for her, but I had already seen the guilty look on her face. I gave it about twenty minutes then went down stairs. I made my way to the disco booth and picked up the mike. 'Ladies and gentlemen, boys and girls, there is a police purge on under age drinking and if they walk in here I am likely to lose my licence so please all underage drinkers please exit the building now, thank you. A few people started to move but there was still a lot that I thought were underage, so I said. 'I still can see faces that go to my daughters school and if they don't move their arses now, I will be forced to come down and embarrass them in front of their friends.' I never realized how many underage drinkers there were, most of them were girls, made up to the nines, some of them could have only been fourteen but with all that shit on their faces they looked eighteen or nineteen, they would get the older ones to buy their drinks for them because as soon as they opened there mouths you could tell they weren't old enough to drink.

Tasha mentioned the following day when she got home from school, that some of her friends asked her, would your dad really have embarrassed us?, Tasha said, you had better believe it.

We had been open about a month when my cleaner came to me and said, "have you taken a picture down in the recess, because one is missing?" I shot round there double quick, one of the big prints was missing, a Black Panther laying on a branch of a tree, it was my favourite, that's it I thought some ones going to pay for this. That night when the pub was full I got in the D.J booth and cut the music half way through a song, that's the best way to get everybody's attention. I said 'I'm going to speak to you in your language, some fucking arshole has stolen a picture from in the recess, now it's not exactly a small picture so someone must have seen whoever took it, I want it back, the company haven't spent a quarter of a million pounds on doing this place up for you lot to turn it into a shithole, if anything else goes missing or gets broken I'm going to put a charge on the door, someone's got to pay for these things and it's not going to be me.' As I've said before there is always one smart arse that has to try it on. Later that week a small picture of Alex Higgins went missing round by the pool table, so that night I was back on the microphone and said, 'from this Thursday through to Saturday there will be a pound charge on the door.' You can't do that someone shouted. 'Watch me' I said, 'you were all warned so don't blame me, blame the thieving twat who keep's nicking my pictures.'

Six thirty Thursday night I stood on the door and collected a pound off every person that came in, there were a few that wouldn't pay, so they never came in, no exceptions, some tried to get in the back door by way of the garden, but I had my spies and they were pointed out to me later, I didn't fuck about, they either paid or they got a slap and kicked out, most of them laughed and paid and said it was worth the try, one or two refused to pay and said they weren't leaving, how wrong they were. Over the following couple of weeks the trade dropped, then for some reason it came back with a vengeance, every night the pub was three quarters full, even on my night off, the older crowd came in, the one's who didn't like disco music, they could play their own songs on the juke box, and had nice and comfortable surroundings to sit in.

At this time the brewery were offering incentives on all machines, if you took over fifty per cent on the previous quarters take you would get a fifty pound bonus, over hundred per cent a hundred pound bonus, this was over every quarter (every four months I was receiving a hundred pound bonus). We also won a day trip on the Orient Express as we grossed the most take in our area, everything was going along nicely, we were also doing mid-day pub meals, the normal run of the mill stuff in those days was chicken and chips, scampi and chips, fish and chips, cottage pie and lasagne. The tables were set out nice with a flower on, yes, every thing was going great. Penny, who was our stand in cook was also helping behind the bar this particular day, when someone informed me there was smoke coming from the kitchen, I shouted 'Pennyeeeeee,' and we both rushed to the kitchen at the same time to see the chip pan was on fire. 'Give me your apron' I said, she was fast, it was in my hand before I reached the sink, the apron was much bigger than the tea towels so I soaked it and laid it across the chip pan, I then wet some tea towels and did the same, it could have been worse if somebody hadn't noticed it when they did, Penny was in tears and couldn't apologise enough. 'Accidents happen penny' I said, 'at least your not pregnant.' she stopped crying, "What's that got to do with it?" she said. 'Accidents happen' I said and walked away. It took her mind of the mess in the kitchen for a while and when she came back into the bar she asked me what I meant by that remark in the kitchen. 'Nothing' I said, 'I just didn't like seeing you cry so I put a different thought in your head.' Penny stayed in my employment for quite some time; she ended up having her own pub for a number of years called the Wishing Well.

CELEBRITES

My pub was directly in front of Bletchley Leisure Centre. One Saturday afternoon I was serving behind the bar when I noticed a face that I had seen many times on T.V. When he had taken his seat I wondered over to him and introduced myself as the governor of the pub. He didn't seem to impressed, but when I told him that Bomber Pat was a personal friend and colleague of mine he seemed to take an interest. "Is that right?" he said. What's your name?" he asked and when I told him he said, "Yes, Pat had mentioned you." Now I thought he was taking the piss but then he said, "Pat came and opened this place for you didn't he?" 'That's right' I said. So now I must assume that Pat did say something. "I don't live that far from here he said, and Pat had said if he didn't finish too late he would call in and see me, he also said that you and he worked in Germany together if I'm not mistaken." He went on to say, he plays squash at the leisure Centre whenever he can and would call in again. I thanked him, and told him I would keep as many people as I could from pestering him, Kevin Whately (of Auf Wirdersehen Pet, Morse, and of late, Lewis.) became a regular customer.

Johnny Kincaid

A friend of mine who we shall call Smirnoff because he liked his V.A.T (vodka and tonic) came in one night with a couple of new faces. "John he said, I would like to introduce you to Graham a friend of mine who I haven't seen for a long time, he's been touring with a group as their roadie," 'Nice to meet you I said, did you enjoy being on the road and doing all that travelling, because I loved it, living out of a suit case for a couple of months, different hotels, meeting different people every day, was you travelling abroad or was you moving around this country all the time? "We were abroad most of the time" he said. 'Great I said and was this band you travelled with famous, would I know them? I asked, "Maybe if your into heavy rock" he said. 'Not really' said I. "Have you ever heard of Deep Purple? He said, 'Of course who hasn't?' "Well that's who I work for" said he. 'Right' said I For some reason not believing him, anyway we changed the subject and we all enjoyed the evening. That night I was in one of my late night moods, so I kept a few of my regulars back for a knock-out pool match, the friend of Smirnoff said his boss likes a good game of pool, would it be alright if he brings him down on Saturday? 'Be my guest' I said, 'and if he likes he can stay for a private game after we close.' "I'm sure he would like that" he said. As usual Saturday night was buzzing, the atmosphere was nice and light everybody seemed in a good mood. Smirnoff caught my eye so I wondered over to him, he was grinning all over his face, "Johnny boy I would like you to meet Ian Gillan." 'Hello' I said shaking his hand 'welcome to Kincaid's,' then the penny dropped, Ian Gillan the lead singer of

Deep Purple. I looked at Smirnoff's friend and said, 'I owe you an apology because I thought you were getting me at it the other night. That night we had a late drink, now I'm not a big head but I can play a decent game of pool and at a cost I found out so could Ian. To cut a long story short he kicked my arse, as the saying goes, but every dog has his day and mine came the following weekend, but Ian was that good I invited him to join our pool team, which he did. I cant sing (excuse the pun) Ian's praises enough, because at the time we were trying to raise money to buy a mini bus and have it converted to take a couple of wheel chairs for the mentally and physically handicapped school. We held a fete-day, with a bucking bronco, various games, and Ian auctioned one of his platinum discs, he also played pool for a pound for charity and if any one beat him he would put a fiver in the pot. On the day, we needed to raise eleven hundred pounds to go with the rest we had raised to make up the sum amount for the mini bus; we made twelve hundred and seventy pounds. The following week Ian came down and presented the cheque to the Mayor, and the mayor presented the cheque to the representative of the school. The most money taken at one time was for Ian's platinum disc, which went for just under five hundred pounds, and my old mate Smirnoff is the proud owner of that disc.

Smirnoff, my mate the proud owner of Ian Gilans Platinum Disc

Ian is a character and we had many laughs together. It was coming up Christmas time and Ian phoned to say he couldn't make it on this certain day, so Smirnoff and myself took the road to Cublington. Smirnoff was driving because I had to hold the drinks. On arrival at the Manor Ian was quite surprised to see us. 'If Mohamed won't come to the mountain, the mountain will have to come to Mohamed. Merry Christmas and here's your drink, I never forgot your wife either, here's her Guinness, pulled with my own fair hand" I said. "You're a darling" she said, "take a seat or go into the kitchen and help yourself to the mince pies." I made my way to the kitchen were I found she had made enough mince pies to feed an army, one or two wont go amiss, I thought, so I had about four, I'm a pig for mince pies.

I'm sure Ian wont mind me telling this story that he told to me when he first moved into the area. He took a walk up to the village pub where he encountered a few yuppies. "Hello" one said to him, looking him up and down. There was Ian dressed in normal casual attire, jeans, jean jacket, bandana. "It's fairly quite around here you know", still looking him up and down. "That's nice" Ian said in his best-cultured voice, "I live at the bottom of the Manor" the yuppie said. "That's nice for you," said Ian, "and where have you moved to if you don't mind me asking," said the yuppie. "I have just brought the Manor and you could be on my land." "Oh," said the yuppie turning back to his friends. Ian said, "John you should have seen his face it was a picture. Later that day he showed me around the Manor. I cant remember how many acres of land he had, but the house itself, you could get lost in. He took me into his trophy room. Other than his gold, silver, and platinum discs hanging everywhere, in a corner there was stacked a pile of Christmas presents and in the centre of the room was a desk, a child's desk. "Look" he said, "have a look at that, the top lift's up, look at the joins, dovetail joints" he said, and with great pride he said, "I made that." Never mind all the money he had spent on his little girl for Christmas, he was so proud that he had made something for her with his own hands, that must have been around twenty one years a go, and I wouldn't mind betting, that desk is still in the family somewhere.

Johnny Kincaid

During my time at Kincaid's they had a number of Managers running the Bow Bell pub, but for some reason they just wouldn't stay there. I was asked if I would consider running both the Kincaid and the Bow Bell's together. I said I would consider it and discuss it with my other half. We both agreed that it could further my career in the pub game, so I said I would run it for a year on the agreement that I would earn bonuses from both houses, which they excepted. Jean mainly looked after Kincaid's and as the Bow Bell had been run down for so long I spent a lot of time over there getting things up and running again. It was nice that three quarters of the punters were glad to see me back, the rest were only the ones that I had barred the last time I was there. I told them all, they know what I'm like, I'm fair, if they play up they get two public warnings, then their disqualified, which means there out the pub for good but the ones that had already been disqualified by me the first and second time around don't get any public warnings, one fuck-up and their out, if they show me and the pub respect they will get shown respect back, but if they cant do that, it would be better they find somewhere else to drink. In the year that I spent back at the Bow Bell's only one of the original crowd I had to Bar.

I took the Bow Bell back to it's former height's of having quiz nights and disco's, live singer's on a Saturday night, and arranging weekend trips to Amsterdam or Hamburg. The hardest time I had there was the Christmas and New year period, running backwards and forwards to Kincaid's to sort out trouble.

For instance this particular night two lads had decided to have a fight on the dance floor. I arrived just as they grabbed each other and fell to the floor, one of the lads had long greasy hair, the other had fairly long hair with sideburns, the one with the greasy hair was underneath so I walked forward and slipped my foot off of his head and pinned his hair to the floor, I then grabbed the others hair and by putting my elbow between his shoulder blades I wrenched his head back as far as it would go, I then spoke to them in a soft and calm voice, 'you are stopping my customers from enjoying themselves and dancing, now if you really want to fight I have a nice big garden out side, by all means carry on out there, but not on my fucking dance floor,"

The one underneath was shouting for me to get off of his hair. I told him to shut the fuck up. I was looking into the eyes of the one on top when I said, " I'm going to let you go, but if you make a move to punch or kick this guy I will break your arm or leg, which ever one you attempt to use, and you know I can, and will, so I want you to get straight up and walk out to my garden, do you understand?' He kind of grunted his acknowledgement, as he stood up I came up with him just in case he made a move on me, but I still had a foot on the other guys hair, who at this point was trying to remove it. I told him to stop or I would make him look a bigger fool than he already was. I also told him if he wants to continue the fight to follow the other guy out into the garden and if he wanted I would referee, if not please leave the premises, because if he stayed there would be friction in the air and it would create a bad atmosphere. I then lifted my foot and released his hair, he jumped to his feet and gave me one of those if only looks. I looked him straight in the eyes and smiled, the ball was in his court. Did he try his luck with me or finish what was started with the other guy? He made the right decision; he turned and walked to the garden. I stood at the garden door and watched them shape up, they were circling one another when someone tried to push pass me. 'Where do you think your going?" I said. "That's my mate out there" he said. 'Fine' I said, "give me fifty pence." "What the fuck for?" he asked. 'Well you normally pay to watch a boxing or a wrestling match, unless you were thinking of joining in, and believe me my friend that's just not going to happen.' The two guys had stopped circling each other and one enquired what was going on. By this time there were a few wanting to get out in the garden, so I told them I was charging people to watch them fight. I couldn't hear what was said between them, but they both came back into the bar with out throwing another punch.

My year at the Bow Bell was nearly up and the last bonus quarter of the year was fast approaching, I knew that the first two quarters I never reached my target figures but we had such a good last quarter that I had passed the target figures half way through the third month. My staff and I had worked our bollocks off, we ran darts tournaments, pool tournaments, quizzes, fun-days for kids, fun-days for adults, hen-nights, strippers nights, Karaoke nights, discos, we even had auction nights, that's when you bring something from home, put a price on it, if we reach the price you want, you take the money and everything over that price goes to charity.

Can you imagine my surprise when receiving my wages at the end of the quarter to find there was no bonus added? I had already promised my staff a share of it; in fact I had been contemplating signing on for another year. I had trained up a girl as assistant manager and she had the respect of all the customers, so I had the opportunity to spend more time at the other pub with Jean.

I quickly contacted my new area manager to find out what was wrong and why I never got my bonus from the Bow Bell. He told me that when he took over the area he was told that I was running it on a temporary basis and there was no mention of bonuses anywhere. "Have you got a contract, or was it a verbal agreement? He asked. 'A verbal agreement' I replied. "Then they don't have to pay you a penny" he said. I was so shocked that I couldn't speak without saying a swear word in every sentence. I apologised afterwards and told him I didn't mean to take it out on him. The following day I made arrangements to meet the area-managing director who couldn't see me until the following week because of business commitments, or was it to give me time to cool down.

The meeting went much as I expected, nice and casual like to start with, coffee was offered and accepted, we were on first name terms and we spoke about everything in general, except my problem. I could see he was waiting for me to broach the subject so I kept him waiting no longer. 'Well Phil bottom line I said. I

Johnny Kincaid

have been a loyal employee of this company for a good number of years and I have run one or two rough pubs that nobody else would touch with a barge poll, one such pub is the Bow Bell, when I took over that pub I had an agreement that if I hit the targets I would receive bonuses on both pubs, so why do I get only one bonus for Kincaid's and nothing for the Bow Bell? My staff and I worked our backsides off to bring that pub back up from the pits.' Before I could say another word he jumped in with, "well Mr Kincaid", I thought to myself here comes the bullshit, he has dropped the Johnny and started all official with Mr Kincaid. "It's been reported to this office by your present area manager that you told him you had a verbal agreement with Mr Anderson, who was your area manager at the time of this so called agreement, and as you well know he left the company eight months ago." What he was trying to say is that he only has my word that an agreement was made between Anderson and myself. I stopped him right there and said, 'don't say another word, tomorrow you will have something in black and white on your desk, my resignation.' As I turned to leave, he said. "If that's the way you feel." I spun around quick, which took him by surprise because he fell back on to his seat. 'I told you not to say another word, I'm on a short fuse and I will deck you before anyone got in to this office. I've been shafted and I don't like the feel of it, so my advice to you is, please! Don't say another word.'

I left the office and walked the whole length of the corridor expecting to hear him screaming after me, or to see the security guards coming towards me, but there again I hadn't touched him, so there could be no assault charge this time, only I know how close he came to being floored, maybe not, maybe that's why he never left his office. The following day I typed and sent my resignation, stating that I was giving one months notice and as from today I would not be opening the Bow Bell public house either, however I did go there to put a notice in the windows that the pub would be closed until further notice. When I sent my resignation into the office, I only put a second class stamp on the envelope so it would take a couple of days to get there, so unless the area manager or someone from the office got in touch with me, there pub was going to lose a couple of days trading. I'll teach them to penny pinch, the tight bastards.

A few months prior to the episode over the bonuses I was in the London Pride having a drink with the governor when his area manager came in. John Taylor introduced me and a big smile came across his face. Of cause, Mr Kincaid, I have heard a lot about you in the trade and I have seen you on many occasions at Wembley Town Hall, you see I'm a wrestling fan and I came into the Bow Bell when you first took it over but you were to busy to talk. We spoke about wrestling for approximately fifteen minutes then I made a polite excuse to get away, but before I had finished my drink he offered me one of his cards and said if ever I was unhappy where I was I could always give him a call. I thanked him, and with a smile on my face I said, "but could you afford me? "We would break the bank to get someone like you Mr Kincaid he said", "you must be highly thought of by your company to rename one of there prestigious pubs after you, I don't know of another pub in England which is named after a living person." On that note I had to leave other wise my head would never have got through the door.

I'm not a person for keeping cards but for some reason I kept his, they say there is always a reason for everything, and now I know what the reason was. At the time I was very happy in what I was doing and I could never foresee myself leaving the company I was working for, but as the saying goes, you never know what's around the corner. As I was packing a few things away in the office I came across a little silver box. I had no idea what was in this box or where it came from but to my surprise on opening it the first thing I saw was this guys business card. I had been thinking of moving back home and then maybe getting in touch with a couple of brewery's to see if they needed any managers, or I could always go back to the wrestling as a referee, but that was a non starter as soon as I mentioned it to Jean. There was no way she was letting me go back on the road travelling again, she said since we have been together I had spent over half of it away from her, now's the time to be together with the children. Not only that but also this business card seemed to be cropping up where ever I went. I was sure I left it in the office, yet I found it up stairs on the table by my armchair, then I found it down stairs behind the bar. The strangest time was when I went to pay for my petrol and I pulled the card out instead of my credit card. Was someone trying to tell me something? I made the phone call, and within one week I was looking at a pub in Watford. It was one big beautiful pub with an eighty-seater restaurant, it also had a massive great garden with loads of kiddies' swings and toys, this was the kind of pub that any manager would give his high teeth for. Do you like it? The area manager kept asking. "Do you really like it?" he said, I was getting a little bit suspicious. 'Why do you keep asking if I like it' I said. 'What's there not to like about it, or is there something your not telling me? I enquired. "No" he said, "the pub is yours if you really want it, but before I left the office this morning I saw on the computer that another one of our pubs became vacant in Milton Keynes, now I don't want you to sign for this pub then find out there was a pub in Milton Keynes that you would rather have taken because it's nearer your home, and then think I was trying to do the dirty on you, I'm being straight, out of the two, this one has the greater potential, but if you would like to look at the other one and talk it over with Jean, I will meet you there tomorrow and show you around."

"That seems reasonable to me, I said. What's the name of this pub, and where is it in Milton Keynes? "It's on Hodge Lea and the name is the Bradwell Monk," said he.

MY DOGS

It was while I was at the Bow Bell's pub that I came in possession of a bloody great big German shepherd dog. I was told it was about three years old and it was house trained. 'I should hope so if it was three years old,' I said. He's a big old softie I was told but a big old softie is no good to me, I wanted a guard dog, so I had to start training it myself. One day a woman came to me and said that she had just seen her old dog in my back yard, she said that she had to let it go because it got to big for her flat, then she went on to say, does he still have his tea and weetabix in the mornings? 'No' and he don't sleep on the sofa either.' The first night I had him he jumped up on the sofa and I told him to get down, he showed me his teeth, he didn't know what hit him, I cut my knuckles on both hands but he had to learn who's boss, he only ever showed me his teeth once after that and that was when he was having a go at my mongrel dog behind the bar. I was in the office and I heard the barking and snarling and then I heard Jeans voice, well straight away I thought he was having a go at Jean, so I rushed out of the office and into the bar, Jean was stuck in a corner holding a pool cue and Prince was directly in front of her, it wasn't until I was half way along the bar that I saw Bobby my mongrel underneath Prince, I took a swing at Prince with my foot and missed him, but he took off out of the bar and up onto the eye level, where I took chase, did he think I was playing with him because he took off again and I chased him up and down that bloody eye level four or five times, when finally he went under a table, when I bent down to drag him out he snapped at me and caught the side of my hand, the chairs and table went flying and before he could make a move I had him by the scruff of the neck and the back end and he was flying through the air, that wasn't clever and I'm not proud of what I did, but it was more in frustration and temper than anything else, the thought that he was having a go at Jean first, then me not being able to catch him and then the fucker biting me, I'm glad to report nothing like that ever happened again, in fact I'm sure that dog was human sometimes, he did things that I never taught him, like at the end of the evening session and the first bell had rung, he would make his way down stairs come into the bar and parade from one end of the bar to the other, then lay down in the door way, when the second bell went he would do the same again but this time he would lay further in the bar, and my bar staff would have to step over him, I would shout Prince get in! And he would take no notice; I would say again, Prince get in! And he would turn his head the other way, but as soon as I lifted the hatch, he was gone; it was a ritual we had to go though every night.

If I was having a late drink I would let him out into the pub, he would go around and sniff everyone then go and lay up on the eye level and if anyone went near him he would walk away, and if they pursued he would let them know by a little growl to stay away, the only time a person could get near him was if I was by his side, or they had a child with them, he loved kid's, funny that.

We had moved into Kincaid's when one day Cass asked me if I wanted another dog because she had to get rid of it before her old man killed it. 'What is it?' I asked, German shepherd bitch. 'Bring it around and if Prince likes her we will have it' I said.

It was like love at first sight for Prince, I'm not so sure of the thoughts of Kissey, what a name for a dog, that had to be changed, and so it was, to Zara.

Zara was about eight months old and a quick learner, where Prince hadn't seen another dog since he had been with me he was all over her like a rash. I only ever took Prince out late at night or early hours of the morning when there was no other distractions, it was easier to train him then, but now I hoped Zara would learn from him, and she did.

I remember one day when my mate Smirnoff said he could go up to my flat and the dogs wouldn't bother him, because he knew them, but as I said before, I was always with him when my dog's were around. 'Well if you think you can be my guest' I said,

so he came behind the bar, walked through the doorway towards the stairs, the next thing we saw was Smirnoff in full flight running through the bar shouting JOHN!

When the dog's got to the doorway of the bar and saw me they stopped barking, Smirnoff was on the other side of the hatchway, with the door closed. "Their fucking mad" he said, "they were at the top of the stairs looking at me, I spoke to them then I put my foot on the first step and they went fucking mad as if they didn't know me." 'They know you all right, they know you're not allowed up stairs that's my place up there, even the bar staff don't go up those stairs, they call me from the bottom, but they never attempt to go up.'

We had a flat roof to three sides of Kincaid's and I used to let the dogs out onto it, there was a private side entrance and an alley leading to the back garden which the customers shouldn't use, their entrance to the garden was on the other side of the pub. One night Jean was coming down to the bar when she heard a noise outside the back door, as she slowly opened it she saw a pair of shoes pointing down wards, and as she had a closer look there was a guy laying there with Zara by the side of him, "what you doing there?" she asked. "Don't let him bite me" he said, "I was only walking from the garden and he jumped on my back." "You shouldn't have been walking through this way, it says private entrance on the garden gate or cant you read?" "I was taking a short cut" he said and as he went to move, Zara beside him and Prince still on the roof, growled together. "How long have you been there?" Jean asked. "About twenty minutes, every time I went to move they were going to bite me." "So your short cut wasn't so short after all was it?" she said. "You won't be coming this way again will you? Because if you do and this happens again I will leave you here all night," then she told Zara to get in. The guy got to his feet and Jean pointed to the roof, "thank your lucky stars that it wasn't the big one that jumped you, because you wouldn't have any bollocks left now." Jean said the blood just drained from his face and he was gone, she said even Prince would have had trouble catching him.

I had a phone call late one night, "Mr Kincaid" the voice said, "that's right," I said. Sergeant what ever his name was! said, "have you got a couple of German Shepherds? 'Yes I have' I answered, "well their terrorising my police force at the bottom of the Queens way," "your kidding" I said, "I kid you not" he said, "I'm sorry and I'll get them in straight away," I legged it down towards the co-op which was about a quarter of a mile away, when I got there! There was no one around except a lone policeman, "looking for your dog's John" he asked, "there up the other end of the Queens way" he said, "jump in the car and I'll take you up there" thank fuck for that I was already knackered for running down to the co-op, when we arrived up the top end there were about five coppers trying to corner Prince and Zara, I opened the window of the car and shouted GET HOME, the two took of like greyhounds, I apologised to the policemen and enquired if any of them had been attacked, and they ensured me that they hadn't, when I got back to the pub the two dog's were back on the roof, how the hell did they get off of it in the first place, then get back on it, there was only one way and that was jump the ally, and if I never saw it with my own eyes I wouldn't have believed it, across the ally was another flat roof with open stairs going down, so I walked across the ally up the stairs on to the flat roof and called Prince, "come on boy," and with a bit of a run up he cleared the ally with couple of feet to spare, the bastard, I had to erect a small fence all around the bloody roof, more expense.

A year or two later I lost Prince to the common affliction of German Shepard's, arthritis of the hips, I don't mind admitting I cried when he was put down, it was like losing a close friend, I even slept with him on a couple of occasions in the last week of his life, he used to sleep out side our bedroom door, and I would hear him whine when he was laying there and tried to move, so I would take him into the spare room, get a quilt and lay there with him, it was a heart braking decision when we decided to have him put to sleep, but also the kindest thing, as he was in agony.

Zara took it bad as well, she was pinning for him and not eating, I mentioned this to a friend of mine who said his friend had a seven month old German Shepard that he wanted to get rid off, and he would let it go to a good home, it was a beautiful black and tan dog, and scatty as pups go, I could tell he was going to be a big dog by the sizes of his paws, he was seven months old and never been house trained, this is why the other guy wanted to get rid of him, he was shitting all over the place and had ripped his three piece suit to pieces, do you remember that song (here we go again, catch us if you can) well that was me, here I go again, training the little bastard with the help of Zara, and catching the little fucker when he did a runner on me, as I said before I only ever took the dog's out late at night when there was no other distractions around, well this particular night we were over the fields by the canal, when Max my new dog saw a fox, Zara just sat there, she went to go but I said stay and she did, but Max was away, and it didn't matter how much I called him, he kept going, I have always trained my dog's off the lead, but Max became the exception, it took a long time and a lot of patients before I could trust him, and let him off the lead for long periods of time, but he was a character, I taught him to jump over the bar, by whistling and a hand movement, but I didn't teach him to thieve, one day it was pissing down with rain so the dog's were inside, they use to stay in the staff room if the weather was bad, I was leaning across the counter talking to someone when she said I have just seen your dog coming from the off licence, behind me was a doorway, left of the doorway led to my off licence, right of the doorway led to my office and the staff room, I didn't take much notice of what she said but a little later she said there he goes again, this time I turned just in time to see Max disappearing around the corner, I followed him in to the staff room where he went and put his head straight into the corner under the sinks, I called to him, he didn't turn, Max I said with aggression in my voice, he still never turned, so I pulled him back slowly by the tail, and as his head came into view I saw the rapper of a kit-cat in his mouth, you thieving little bastard I said as I took it from him, and as I turned, Zara was laying in the corner by the toilet door with a kit-cat between her paws, he had got one for her then went back for his own, I had to laugh, but I gave his kit-cat to Zara just for the cheek of it.

In total Max gave Zara three litters of pups, and every pup was a gem, the last time she came into season was at the Bradwell Monk Pub, I tried to keep them apart, out side in the yard was a cage where we kept our empty barrels, it had a nine foot wire fence so I put Zara in there out of harms way, Max had the run of the rest of the yard, looking out of the bar window you had a panoramic view of the football pitch, the A5 dual-carriageway, and the round-about coming off the A5, I was looking out when this really flash American motor came round the round-about, I walked closer to the window to get a better look when I happened to look down into my yard, Noooooo I shouted, Max was humping Zara, he looked up without stopping as if to say, to late son, by the time I got down stairs he was stuck, and from that day to this, I will never know how he got in that fucking cage.

They are both gone now, Zara was fourteen and Max was twelve, they both started to suffer with there back-ends at the same time, Max could hardly walk and Zara would drag her back legs after walking about twenty yards, so I laid them to rest at the same time, and I still miss them, who ever said, that a four-legged friend is your best friend, were right

Max and Zara

THE BRADWELL MONK

The infamous Bradwell Monk, I had never heard of the pub or the reputation of the place before I took it, I just fell in love with the pub the first time I set eyes on it, it was so different to all the other pubs I had, let me explain the architecture of the building, as you walk through the double front doors, on the right hand side you had the gents toilets, straight in front of you there was a door that led you to a small function room with a bar, next to this was the ladies toilets, to the far left of this door was another which led you to a massive great bottle cellar which was at least thirty five yards long by fifteen yards wide, this cellar also housed my office, halfway along the right hand wall was another door which led you to the cold cellar, which was about thirty feet by thirty feet wide, when you came back out of the bottle cellar you were at the foot of the stairs which led you up to the bars, there were two flights of stairs, on the first landing there was a massive big picture window that looked out over the front car park, at the top of the second flight of stairs you can either turn left or right, left takes you to the public bar, and right takes you to the lounge and second function room, both bar's had patio doors which led out onto the two football pitches that belonged to the pub, built onto the side of the pub were the changing rooms with showers, you entered the manager's apartment through the first door on the left in the public bar, this contained a kitchen, lounge diner, three bedrooms, bathroom and separate toilet.

The views from the bars were quite astonishing; beyond the football pitches ran the A5 dual carriageway with the slip road coming up to Monks way roundabout, and Bradwell Abby is a short distance away, the Abby had a lot to answer for as you will find out as you read on.

It was soon after we had moved in, I had just finished doing the cellar work and had a shower and was getting dressed when Jean came into the bedroom to ask me something, as she was talking to me the electric Hoover started up in the hall-way, we both looked at each other with a strange grin on our faces, I asked her who was in the flat, "no one" she said, "where's Tasha I asked", "at work" she replied, so who the fuck is using the Hoover, I opened the door with a jolt, there was no one there, the Hoover was a long cylinder type with a button on the end, "you couldn't have turned it of properly" I said, she said she had switched it of by the wall switch, "well it don't switch on by it's self does it, so you couldn't have switch it of properly" said I,

Soon after we were standing in the kitchen talking, I was standing with my back against the up-right fridge freezer, and Jean was leaning against the sink, when all of a sudden the tumble dryer started by it's self, we both turned to look at it, there had to be a logical explanation for it but for the life of me I couldn't think of one, you see, the fucking thing was broke, it didn't work, it was knackered, it was just a lump of junk that the previous landlord had left for me to get rid off, I had to make a joke of it as I was shitting myself, I said who ever it is likes doing the house-work, Hovering and the washing, that was the first and last time that machine ever worked in that kitchen, I had a friend look at it for me and he said it needed a new computer board and it would be cheaper buying a new machine, that wasn't the only time that spooky things happened there, one night I had just gotten into bed, it was a late night, I had a few drinks with friends and then did my book work so the time must have been somewhere around two in the morning, I had just cuddled up to Jean when it felt like someone had sat on the bottom of the bed, trying to keep my voice under control, I said please, I've had a busy old day and I'm very tired so if you don't mind I would like to get some sleep, it was only seconds later as if somebody had stood up and the bed went back to normal, I said good night, and to tell you the truth if I could have got under Jeans skin I would have, I don't think I could have gotten any closer to her if I tried.

They say animals can sense anything paranormal, well I'm sure they can, I was working in my office doing some paper work late one night, I had taken my dogs out for a run and came straight back into the office, I gave the dogs some water and settled down to do some work, when all of a sudden Max let out this awful whine, shut up Max I shouted, he laid down with his paws covering his nose, then Zara started to get agitated, she stood up and started to turn in circles, with that Max stood and darted out of the office followed by Zara, and closely followed by me,

It may have been my imagination, but after all that had happened in the flat and in the office, I don't think so, most nights when I was doing my tills, I would be sitting there waiting for them to reconcile, and I would get the distinct feeling that there was some one or something at the end of the bar watching me, I would start singing to myself or whistling, sometimes both at the same time, or maybe I would play the golf machine and make out I was talking to my caddy, Jean never stayed out with me, she felt safer in the flat,

It wasn't until we had left the pub that we actually found out, that the pub was built on top of an old Monks burial ground, so they weren't there to hurt us or to be mischievous, but they nearly turned a black man white.

The pub it's self was full of lovable rouges, of cause there was a few arsholes but you get them in every pub, there was this one guy called Mad Mick I thought he had taken an instant disliking to me as every time I caught his eye he seemed to be snarling, he came to the bar this particular time and I served him, "I understand your wife has just had a baby is that right," he nodded his head, "boy or girl" I asked, "girl" came the reply, "what have you called her, if you don't mind me asking,"

"Chelsea" he said, "what a lovely name," "do you think so" said he, with a smile coming to his face, "I'm a Chelsea fan and what better tribute is there than

From International Wrestler to Pubs and Punters

naming my daughter after them" he said, "there's none that I can think of" said I, he shook my hand and we've been good friends ever since.

He never got the name Mad Mick for nothing, I was told a few stories about him, none that I could verify myself, and I wasn't stupid enough to blatantly ask him encase he turned on me, but one day I nearly saw him turn, now Mick wasn't a big man in stature, he was thick set but not very tall, he was watching me play on the golf machine when an old friend of mine came in, he came over to me and said "I told you Kincaid the next time I see you I'm going to punch seven kinds of shit out of you", Mick's head dropped and slowly turned to look at the person who was giving me abuse, "outside now Kincaid I'm raring to go" said my friend, with that Mick took a step back, I came straight of the machine, "hello Dave" I said, giving him a big hug, "it's been a long time mate", turning to Mick I said "Mick I would like you to meet one of my best friends", "Dave this is Mick", I swear if I hadn't come of that machine when I did, Dave would be minus a nose or an ear, because Mick was ready to spring.

When I left Kincaid's, I brought along with me the lad who was going out with my stepdaughter Mandy, at one time he was a right little villain, in fact, one time I even got him off a prison sentence by writing a letter to his solicitor which was read out in the court, stating how he was a reliable and trustworthy person, who occasionally looked after my pub and did the banking for me, and as the judge was a wrestling fan who had heard of me, said, if Mr Kincaid has faith in you I will show the same kind of faith, but if you ever let him down and appear in front of me again, you will be sorry, out of the four lads that was standing in the dock he was the only one to walk away, needless to say he was never a friend of there's ever again.

I made Gary assistant manager at the monk, but he took the piss, one time when Jean and I went on holiday he was left to run the pub, on our return I thought he had done a bloody good job as the pub was clean and tidy, my stock was all in order and I didn't have any deficits, it was a week or so later when he handed in is notice, over the break down of his feelings for Mandy, he said he had to leave,

It wasn't until two months later when my area manager came to me and asked me to over-bank a thousand pounds, "sure I said, but why", "because you under-banked a thousand pounds two months ago" he said, "I have never under-banked any money since I've been with the company " I said, then he produced a counter foil from the post office bank book, and the takings and banking sheet we have to send in each week, "I beg to differ" he said, as he gave them to me, I sensed there was something wrong but my mind was racing, then it hit me, the date, "we were on holiday on this date, and my assistant manager was running the pub" I said,

"Was the assistant manager appointed by you to do the holiday relief" he asked, "he was" I replied, "then the onus is on you to repay the loss of company money,

If the company had appointed the holiday relief it would be down to them," he said,

We sat in the office for nearly an hour looking at the books, then we came across it, he was good, very good, the way he got the money out, even the area manager said he must have spent a sometime reconciling the figures to get them to correspond like that, he must have known that it would take a month or two before the post office would send the counter foil to head office to marry up with the paper work, and that is when the discrepancy was likely to be found.

I had to repay the thousand pounds, and I put the word out I wanted to see Mr C,

Shortly after wards I heard that he had moved to London, but one day, you never know, our paths may cross again.

About four hundred yards up the road from the Bradwell Monk stood an O.A.P's home, and apparently over the last couple years they have had a lot of trouble with some of the lads leaving the pub, so one night after the disco I took the mike and made an appeal, I said I wanted to get together a committee to raise money for an O.A.P's Christmas party, because god willing we will all get there one day, and it would be nice for someone to do the same for us, I also said it's not just for the home up the road, if anyone has a relative they want to bring they are welcome, there were so many hands went up to be on the committee, I picked Mad Mick to be chairman, and left it to him to pick the rest, and as strange as it might seem we never had any more complaints from the home, I brought the first lot of raffle prizes so the fund had a good start off, we had over forty seven pensioners at the party, there were only two in wheelchairs, and it was a sight for sore eyes to see two of the hardest men around pushing wheelchairs up the back ramp dressed in tux and bow ties.

The money the committee collected covered all the food and drinks, and there was enough money over to put a fiver in each of their Christmas cards, the boys had done well, raising just over five hundred pounds, in total we had fourteen lads running around getting food for the ones that couldn't get around so well, and they all joined in the sing along songs, it was a great day for the young as well as the old, it just goes to show, some of the hardest have hearts of gold.

The worst night I had at the Monk was on a disco night, the first bell had sounded and I had just come in to the public bar when I saw these two guys shaping up to one another, "what the fucks going on here" I shouted, one of the fellas I knew the other one I had never seen before, I came from behind the bar and stepped in between them, the one I knew I pushed back and said "stay there," as I turned to the other one he threw a punch which caught me on the side of the face, I said "not good enough me old son I'm still standing, my advice to you is fuck off now while you still can," with that he threw another punch which I blocked and hooked his arm up his back and put him in a chicken wing, which is a submission hold in wrestling, any sensible person wouldn't struggle because they are likely to hurt themselves, but this silly bastard twisted to his right and pulled his own shoulder out, I am thankful that he never turned to his left, he would have broken his neck, we called a ambulance for him and off he went. The time was two forty five and I was In bed, the phone was ringing and there was shouting out side, I put my dressing gown on and went to the window, there was three police officers below me, "can I help you gentlemen" I said, "Mr Kincaid" one of them asked, "that's me" I said, "could we have a word with you please", "give me a sec and I will be right down", as I opened the front door they were in, "Mr Kincaid I am arresting you for Assault" said the main man, then he went into the legal spill, when he had finished, I said "fine gentlemen, now if you don't mind I'm going back up stairs to get dressed then I will come with you", one put his hand on my arm and I stopped dead and looked at him, "if I wanted to do a runner do you really think I would have let you in, so there really is no need to man handle me", the guy in charge gave the fella who was holding my arm the nod and he let go, when I had taken a few step's I said "by the way, that was the wrong way to hold an arm, it could have been broken so easily" before I entered the bedroom I shouted to Jean to put a dressing gown on as we had visitors, when she opened the door she looked shocked, what the, "what's wrong" she asked, "their taking me down the station, I've supposedly assaulted someone, I'll know more when I get down there" I said.

On reaching the police station I was formally charged with assault, I was asked to make a statement of what actually happened, which was nothing like the statement he had made I was told, I was freed on police bail and advised to see a solicitor, which obviously I did, I gave the solicitor six name's that could verify what had happened that night, the same six name's that was mentioned in my statement, out of the six only two was willing to make a statement of what they saw, three said they didn't see anything because they weren't looking my way when it went off, and the guy who was having the ruck was wanted by the police, so he had done a runner not to be seen, I was summoned to the Magistrates court the following week, where after listening to the prosecutor they referred it to Aylesbury Crown Court, this is bollocks I said to my brief, I was only defending myself, but I should have known better, there is no such thing as self defence in this country, if I was attacked buy fifteen people and I hurt one of them, I'm the one that would be nicked, don't ask me why, but that's the law in this stupid country, it took just over a year to go though the court, (I will explain what happened a little later).

Roy an old mate of mine came in to see me one day, he said he had been looking at a bar in Spain and wanted a partner, he asked if I would be interested, "maybe" I replied, "where about's in Spain" I enquired, "a little place between Torremolinos and Malaga called Arroyo, I'm going to take a look at it next week, and if your interested you can come with me," I told him to book another ticket, either way it would give me a break from the pub for a day or two.

From Malaga airport by taxi it took just under fifteen minutes to arrive outside the Eastenders bar, which was smack bang next to another bar called the Royal Oak, "you've got to be kidding me Roy, two English bars smack bang next to each other, why do you think one of them is up for sale, does to much competition spring to mind, unless you have it in mind to do something entirely different to what your neighbour is doing! Forget it,"

"Shall we take a look inside" Roy said "or have you made up your mind already," "I'm trying to be positive about things, and speak as I see, so we know what we're getting ourselves into" said I,

The inside was in fairly good shape, it needed a bit of paint here and there but on the whole it was in good decorative order, there was a picture on the wall of the Queen Vic, and various photos of the stars in the show, the Bar was situated on the left as you entered from the front door, the Bar its self was around fifteen foot long with steps going up into another room, it had a smaller room which you got to from behind the Bar presumably a kitchen or a rest room, after having a good look around, we took a walk around the immediate area, back on the road we turned right and about three hundred yards up on the left hand side was Arroyo train station, we turned right again and followed the main drag all the way down to the sea, which took about fifteen minutes, but this you must remember is walking down a fairly steep hill all the way, it was a bastard walking back up it, I wanted to get a taxi, but Roy wanted to stop in a few Bars to see what they were like and maybe get a few ideas, when we eventually got back to the Eastenders we bumped into the governor of the

Royal Oak, Roy introduced himself as the prospective new buyer of the Eastenders, within twenty minutes you would have thought they had known each other for donkey's years, but Roy was like that, everyone felt at ease in is company, and like Roy he too was a long distance lorry driver before taking a Bar, but what I notice most was that every person that came into his bar while we were talking were Spanish, I asked him if there were many English in this part of town, and if there were, where did they drink,

He was honest and said, there was a fair amount of English around but this area was predominately Spanish, and if you spoke Spanish it would be a big advantage, well I never spoke a word of Spanish and as far as I new neither did Roy or Carol, I wrestled in Spain and learnt to count to ten, that was my limit, I wasn't very good at picking up languages so I sussed there and then, that this adventure, wasn't going to be for me.

Roy did get himself a partner, Kempy his old sidekick, I went over for their opening night, as I said, I used to wrestle in Spain, so Roy put up a picture and a poster advertising that I would be there, I'm not saying his place was packed out because I was there, maybe it something to do with the fact that the guy next door closed his Bar so as to give Roy a good opening night.

Unfortunately Roy's business only lasted three years, first Kempy came home, and then Roy followed a couple of years later.

Mean while back at the pub, an old area manager came to see me (Danny Hobden) and asked how I was getting on with this company, I said "great, it's just some of the customers I have lost respect for", "Johnny" he said, "I've been given back the Milton Keynes patch and I have two pubs I need managers for, if you want you can take your pick of either of them" "I have great respect for you Danny, but I couldn't work for a company that shafts their managers I said, "put it down to experience, you will never get caught like that again, just make sure you always get something in writing, now do you want to look at these pubs or not" he said, I thought to myself there's no harm in having a look, any way Danny was always straight with me, "ok Dan" I said, "show me the way",

The first pub we looked at was the Blacksmith Arms on Downs Barn, a very nice pub which did food, the pub it's self had a very nice layout, split into two sections, a comfortable Lounge dinning area, and a public bar with pool table and dart throw, I was interested in the food side as long as I could have it on a franchise, but Danny said there was no way they would agree to that, because the food was doing so well, he gave me the figurers on the wet sales (drinks) and on the dry sales (food) and what I could expect as wages, I just laughed, and said "let's have a look at the next pub shall we", in the car he asked me why I laughed, and I said "Danny if I afford you that pub and you knew how much work you would have to put in to generate that kind of take, would you except such a low wage, I think not, or was you waiting for me to haggle over the wages, I don't haggle

Danny, and if that's all you think I was worth, is it worth looking at the next place", Danny apologised, he said he was sincerely sorry, and I believed him, he said it was the business way of doing things, they start with the lowest figure and if it's excepted all well and good, if not they haggle and come to a compromise, but they have a figure that they wont pass, "but I should have known better when dealing with you he said, we have known each other for a long time and I should have given you the top line straight off", then he told me the top line for the Blacksmiths, it was good, but without the food franchise I wasn't interested, we then arrived at the White Hart in west Bletchley, again a nicely set out pub, a massive great lounge that wasn't being used, an L shaped public bar with two fruit machines, a pinball table and a darts throw, down a long corridor to the pool room that had five pool tables, Danny said "before you ask, no it doesn't do food", the wet take was nowhere near what the Blacksmiths was taking, he then told me what the top line was, I didn't say a word just nodded and shook my head, he was telling the truth, "let's see the rest of the place shall we" I said

As we walked up the stairs to the flat, the wall paper was flapping of the walls as we walked pass, the carpet on the stairs was thread bare, and as we entered the flat there was this bloody awful smell, "what the fuck is that smell Dan" I asked, "they had a couple of small dogs that I guess never went out" he said, "Danny, you wouldn't bring your family in to something like this, please don't ask me to bring mine here", "no, your right I wouldn't, and I wouldn't ask you to bring yours in here either, not the way it stands at the moment, you must know someone in the decorating trade who could do this for you, I will arrange for the carpet in here and on the stairs to be laid, if you can arrange the decorating side of it, get who ever to submit two invoices, one high, and one not so high, but it must incorporate the loss of your bonus if you get my meaning" he said, a smile came to my face, "we cant let them get away with that can we" he said, I'd forgotten Danny was a pub manager for a number of years before becoming an area manager.

Area managers, that were once pub managers make the best kind of Area managers, because they have been there in the front line, and know how hard it is to run and maintain a successful pub, a good majority of area managers have never worked behind a bar in their lives, and would shit themselves at the first sign of trouble, personally I think all area managers should be trained for at least a month as bar staff in a well established rough house, so they could see and appreciate what most pub manager go through every week end, most of them never believe you when you tell them this happened or that happened, they all ways come back with well why didn't you try this or why didn't you try that, as if you hadn't, and was waiting for them to mention it, if you had done something generally wrong like breaking one of the company rules, an ex pub manager would give you a short sharp bollocking and leave it at that, you had done something wrong and got caught, your fault for getting caught, don't do it again, that's exactly what Danny was like, I never knew one manager that never liked him, he was very fair.

I asked Danny if I would have a free hand to do what I liked with the White Hart if I took it, and he assured me I would. I told him I would think about it, talk with my other half and let him know within a few days, Jean wasn't to comfortable at the Monk so she agreed to the move. I spoke to Danny and told him I had given my company a months notice and when would it be possible to get the decorators in. As soon as you like was his answer, so I arranged for Danny to pick up the invoices the following day, when he looked at them he said there shouldn't be any problem getting the money paid, I then arranged for the decorators to go in over the week-end and they assured me they would be finished by the following Tuesday at the latest.

Over the next few weeks my friend had his money for decorating the pub, of which he paid me my money, (for my bonus,) the stairs and the lounge had been re-carpeted, and Jean had packed most of our things in boxes, I think I can honestly say that the Bradwell Monk is the only pub that I wasn't to sad to be leaving.

THE WHITE HART

The White Hart (or the Harts as it was known) was a lively pub with lots of so called villains in, by villains I mean people who were legends in their own minds, people who thought they were gods gift to what ever, but most of them were right nice guys that were out for a laugh, I inherited three bar-maids, two young girls and an older woman called Sylvia, Sylvia was a darling, she new her job inside-out, she was always laughing and joking with the customers, that's what you call a real bar-maid,

I once made the mistake of telling her about this Indian Jehovah witness that followed me where ever I went, what ever pub I moved to she would find me. I was playing pool this particular day when Sylvia shouted over to me, "John! The Jehovah witness." I unashamedly threw down the pool cue, dived to the floor and did the commando crawl all the way to bar, as I went through the hatch on my belly Sylvia said "I only wanted to know if she was a red Indian or a Pakistani one," she had the bar in fits of laughter, it took a long while for me to live that one down.

I was having a late drink one night with Sylvia, her husband Roy and a few of his mates, when this other geezer appeared from nowhere. 'Can I help you my friend?' I said. "A pint of lager" came the reply. 'Where have you just come from? ' I asked. "The toilet! I have just woke up" he said. "I think you had better go home" I said, as I walked from behind the bar. "I practise Karate, its better than that phoney shit you call wrestling" he said. Now I'm thinking to myself, do I really need this, this time of night. I took his arm, spun around and took his legs away and ran his face into the carpet. 'Your Karate didn't help you much did it"? I said. His answer was, he wasn't ready. I helped him up and walked him to the door, 'good night my friend, see you tomorrow god willing,' I bade him fare well, as I closed the door the lads at the bar stood there clapping their hands, then one of them said, very diplomatic, you knock the guy down, you pick him up, walk him to the door, you say good night to him, and god willing you will see him tomorrow, now that's diplomacy at its best. I gave them that knowing smile and said, 'I bet he comes back tomorrow or the next day to apologise, because although I showed him up I never barred him and I was pleasant to him, now he will be thinking to himself that he was the one out of order and by rights he should have been barred, on the other hand if I had picked him up and kicked his arse out the door and he went to the police, I would be done for assault, there was a method in my madness" I said.

As it happened he did return a couple of days later, not to apologise but to complain that his wife was not amused, pointing to his face where the carpet burns were scabbed up on his forehead, nose and chin. 'Was she really mad?' I asked. "Fucking right she was, she said she wouldn't be walking out with me looking like that." 'I wouldn't worry about it I said, at least she's talking to you, can you imagine what she would have been like if the burns were on your knees instead of your face? He stopped to think about that one then burst out laughing. 'Let me give you some advise pack in the karate, because you just don't seem to be get the hang of it,' again he laughed, turned, walked to the bar and ordered a beer.

For some reason not known to me the lounge was never used although it was a good size, it also had an eye-level seating area which could be used as a stage, and in the corner stood a disco booth.

One day a guy came to me and asked if I had a room where he and his band could practice, I showed him the lounge and he said it was perfect. I said to him I would make a deal with him, I wouldn't charge him for the use of the lounge, if after a fortnight I opened up and let the punters in, and if any of the punters were musicians they could use your equipment after you had finished your practice, and what I will do is charge a pound entrance fee, and give you all the proceeds for the wear and tear of your gear, he agreed, and within a month I had several bands practicing there, in fact each band brought their own punters along to listen to them practice. I was taking a small fortune on the door which was all going to the group who's equipment was being used, they were earning more money than they would if they were doing a gig.

Johnny Kincaid

Now the pub was getting known for its live music, so I approached one of the better bands that practiced there and asked them if they would to do a live gig for me a fortnight later on a Saturday, I would do all the advertising, and pay them an agreed amount, they would be the first group to play a proper set there for at least fourteen years. The Killer Bees went down a storm, the place was packed, and I had to work myself, as we didn't have enough staff, we still charged a pound on the door, which paid the group and put some money in the kitty for the Christmas Bash.

I still ran the Jam sessions on Wednesdays but now I paid the band a fixed amount, Fridays we held a disco night and Saturdays was live music, one week Rock music the following would be heavy metal, we had Jazz, the Blues, even Country &Western, we catered for everybody and the place was buzzing, we never had doormen and we didn't need them, the only trouble we had was from the neighbours, one lot that lived right next door to the pub called the police on me one night because of the noise, and the police brought with them the noise abatement lot from the council who in turn informed me that I was slightly over the noise decibels for that time of night, they also informed me that they would be back the next day to inform me of alternate ways of dealing with music noise, (I couldn't wait, more bureaucrat red tape). The following morning I knocked on my neighbours door with full intensions of having a right go at them for calling the police but when this young slip of a girl came to the door holding a baby my fury subsided. 'Hi I said, I'm the governor of the pub next door and I believe you sent the police around to see me last night?' "Yes I did she said, the noise was so loud that everything was vibrating on my walls and shelves, I couldn't even put the baby down because she kept waking up." 'What can I say, I'm sorry, but in future instead of calling the police call me, and I will make sure the music is turned down and the base is not loud enough to vibrate your house,' I gave her my number and invited her and her husband in for a free drink Saturday afternoon as a good will token, she thanked me with a big gorgeous smile, steady John, she's married and got a kid I thought to myself.

The chaps from the council arrived in the afternoon, they had some brilliant ideas, soundproof the whole pub, (pillocks) double glaze the windows, (Idiots, as if that would stop the vibration of the base music) or fit a gadget that will cut of the electric to the equipment when it gets to the maximum level of noise aloud, (now their talking). I said 'I would have to consult with my area manager.' We will give you a month, and then if the work has not been done we will pull your music licence. I could have easily punched the smarmy bastard on the nose, it was just the way he said it like, you maybe big and strong, but I have more power. I think if he had said another word I would have punched him but then his partner took over, "I'm sure it wont come to that Mr Kincaid, and I'm sure you will resolve this as quick as possible, but remember your licence is up for renewal next year and you really don't want your neighbours contesting it do you?" 'I'm sure the work will be done as soon as my area manager hears about it," he then took me to one side away from his mate, " you visited one of your neighbours this morning which was a smart thing to do, but there is another one to the back of your property that has sent in complaints of behaviour and loud noise, and with a wink, he said, try and get him on side, and I'm sure you won't have any more problems." Now this is the kind of guy I can work with, by rights he should never indulge where complaints come from, he either liked me or he had it in for the guy on the end bungalow at the back, I thanked him, shook his hand and they both left, later the following day I typed out a letter to the immediate local residents and copied it five times, basically the letter said the same as I said to the girl next door, with my phone number typed in bold, I then proceeded to post them to the two houses past the next door neighbours house, and then to the two houses and bungalow at the back end of my pub car park, I tried to talk to the old boy in the bungalow but he was having none of it, as far as he's concerned the pub should not be there, he had lived there for eight years, the pub had been there for thirty odd. Months later on a Saturday night I had a phone call from him to turn down the music or he would call the police, I never had a band this particular night because Status Quo was playing at the Milton Keynes Bowl and as we were only two miles from the Bowl, if the wind was blowing in the right direction you could open your door and think they were playing in your front room, so I said to the old boy, 'please phone the police and tell them that the band at the Bowl are disturbing my customers, with that I put the phone down, by this time we had the gadget fitted that regulated the noise level and my next door neighbour was happy with it, her house was no more than fifteen feet away from my side wall, the old boys place was at the end of my car park and my car park was sixty-five feet long. It was about five months later when my music licence had to be renewed, so myself and the area manager were summoned to a council meeting, when the meeting eventually got around to me, the chairman asked if there were any objections to the White Hart having a music licence. Sitting about four rows in front of me was this elderly woman and the old boy from the bottom of my car park, the old woman gave the old boy such a dig that it nearly knocked him of his seat. "Can you speak up a bit said the old chap as I'm hard of hearing." Well the crafty old bastard I thought, he's making out his deaf, so if he can hear the music it must be loud, he did a pretty good job on making out he's deaf by every so often asking the chairman to speak up, sorry sir I can't hear you, eventually it was my turn to speak, I explained that we have had over a period of time a number of complaints concerning the loudness of the music, and I have complied with the council ruling to have a decimal counter fitted, I have been to many of my local residents including my next door neighbour who lives less than fifteen feet away from my lounge where the music is played, to get an acceptable loudness and base tolerance, all the neighbours I approached live within fifteen to forty feet from the front of the pub, how Mr Chairman, can a person who lives at the bottom of the car park sixty five feet away and is practically stone deaf hear music that a person fifteen feet away can't, I would say that person must have exceptional hearing or an extra sensitive hearing aid. Within ten minutes I was granted my licence, and we never heard from the old boy again.

The White Hart became known for its music, it was the place to be on a Saturday night, we had very little trouble there, I had more trouble stopping the shagging than stopping fights, someone would come to me and say they had just seen a fella go into the ladies toilets, so off I would go and spoil someone's fun, I can understand a girls frustration when all she wants is a pee, and there's a girl in the next toilet screaming her head off with excitement, I could never understand why then girls never went to the men's toilet, I'll take that back, the smell on a heavy night is enough to put anyone off. I have caught girls sitting on guy's laps shagging, with people sitting next to them. It was a rock and roll night and the guys came as teddy boys, and the girls came in there flared dresses, this particular girl was sitting facing her guy, legs astride his, I took no notice at first but she gave herself away, at first I thought she was just moving to the music, going from side to side and probably trying to wind him up, but then she started to go up and down and she went right out of sync with the music, I hated to do it but I had to stop them, so I wondered over and whispered in her ear, if I can see what your doing so can everybody else, so take your time but get of him, they left soon after, probably to finish off in the car, but then it was his seat getting messed up not mine. The things people do for a dare. It was a Saturday night and the place was buzzing, one of my bar staff came to me and said it would be advisable if I took a walk down to the pool room, I enquired why, "take a look at the c.c.t.v and you will see" she said, I took a slow walk round to the public bar and switched on the c.c.t.v that showed the pool room, and there they were on the end table, she was bent over holding the pool cue and it was so obvious what he was doing by holding on to her hips and making the short sharp movements back wards and forwards, the bar maid that came to get me looked at the screen and said "oh my god." 'Why are you surprised, you're the one who told me about them' I said. "Yes, but that wasn't the same guy that was at it when I came to get you" she said. I legged it down to the pool room, as I entered the room I shouted, 'so who thinks their next?' Some of them probably wondered what the fuck I was on about, but the guys up the far end knew exactly what I was on about, 'right, I'm closing the pool room as from now, put your balls down the holes and I don't mean up the hole and I will re-in burse your money,' there was minimal argument. As the young lady in question passed, I told her I didn't want to see her in the pub again, she gave me one of those who gives a fuck looks, the guy who was doing the dirty was the last to leave. 'What the hell do you think you were doing, you know we have a camera down here and we check on it every so often.' "I know but it was a dare, we dared her to do it knowing there's a camera down here, then we said she couldn't take all of us and she would have if you hadn't come down." I some times still see that girl; she's married now with a baby and looks like butter wouldn't melt in her mouth.

At the moment I can only remember one other thing happening in the Harts, and that was a window being broken, it was on a dance night when one of the hard men of the pub came to me and said that a group of people have just left the pub and one of them had punched a window in as he was leaving. I legged it out side and caught them just as they were getting in their car, just a minute I shouted I want a word with you. The guy who was in the passenger seat got back out and said if it's about your window I'm sorry, but there was this prick in there who was winding me up and I didn't want to fight in there so I got my group together and we were leaving when I just snapped and punched the window, I will be back in a couple of days and pay for it. I was just about to say something to him when the guy who told me about them in the first place butted in, he let off torrent of abuse to them calling them all the names under the sun, one of the women got back out of the car to try and calm him down but she got it as well, I said 'that's enough my old son' and took his arm to lead him back inside, he pulled away, and said "don't touch me or I will chin you as well."

When he woke up I was sitting beside him, "nobody had seen what had happened and that's the way we'll keep it," I said, but I was wrong, across the road lived a girl I had known for a long time who also drank in the pub and who unfortunately was looking out of her window and saw everything, I say unfortunately because when she has had a drink she talks to much, and it wasn't long before everybody was asking me what went on between the two of us. I said I wouldn't say anything and I never did, but when they went to him he naturally thought I had, and came looking to have it out, I said 'what their saying is true, but believe it or not I haven't said a word and if it wasn't for your brother it wouldn't have come to that in the first place, because it was that prick who was winding the guy up, but if you so wish we could always go out side for a return match, if that's what your really looking for lets go for it.' No, no, came the reply, "I just thought we came to an agreement that nothing was to be said and now all the rumours are flying around." It was seven or eight days later when he came to me with an apology, "sorry mate offering his hand, (he had found out who had started the rumour) I was to quick to jump to conclusions." I took his hand and accepted his apology.

THE COURT CASE

I had been backward and forward to the court on a number of occasions and now it was drawing to a close, I wasn't guilty but sitting in that box you start to wonder what it was like sitting there knowing you are guilty of murder and waiting for the verdict to come back and hearing the foreman say, guilty, then hearing those words from the Judge (to be hung by your neck until you are dead) it was frightening and I started to scare myself. The jury were due back in at any time now, as they came back I looked at their faces and I had a strange feeling go through me.

"Will the Foreman of the jury please stand", said the clerk of the court. This podgy little guy with glasses stood up and when he was asked how did they find, his speech kind of came out slow and drawn out. "Guilty as charged" he said. What the fuck does he know, was he there I was thinking to myself, then the judge was rambling on about something or other, taking the law into your own hands, you have to deal with a situation as you see it, if I had done nothing but phone the police. By the time they arrived I would have had a full blown riot on my hands and a wrecked pub, and probably a lot of injured people as well, because friends of the guys who were fighting would have got involved, and probably some innocent bystander would have got a bottle over his head, as I said before he threw the first punch, I then asked him to leave, he then tried his luck again, and I swear to this day I did not pull his shoulder out, he did, he shouldn't have moved.

Conclusion. Governors and Managers of pubs are in a no win situation, if you do things by the book and call the police more than three times, they say you can't control your premises and yet if you do leave the bar area to sought a problem out, your in the wrong if things go tits up. The out come of the court case was I was fined and had to pay compensation to the idiot who hurt himself and then I had to surrender my pub licence within six weeks, in other words I was kicked out of Milton Keynes and couldn't hold a licence within the Buckinghamshire area for the period of five years.

THE ROYAL OAK

It was coming up to five weeks when I had a phone call from a guy called Alex an area manager from Luton. "I understand your looking for a pub, I think I have just the one for you" he said. I didn't really want to go to Luton but as the old saying goes beggars can't be choosers, so off to Luton I went to see this pub, The Royal Oak in Round Green and what a shit hole of a pub it was, there were marks on the wall where pictures once hung, it had an L shaped bar with a pool table at one end, you could never get more than fifty to seventy people in at one time and I'm probably exaggerating at that, the only thing good about the place was the flat up stairs, it was nice and big, and surprisingly clean.

The Royal Oak being a smaller pub than the Harts, and the same brewery owning it I expected them to try and knock my money down, but Alex said I would be on the same money as I was on at the Harts, which surprised me, as you could fit half this pub into the disabled toilets at the Harts.

I hadn't spent a lot of time in the pub before I went to court for my licence, I had only seen the day time customers. On entering the court the licensing officer made himself known to me, "Mr Kincaid so nice to meet you at long last, when your finished in there please come to my office" which he pointed to along the corridor, "I would like a word with you if that's ok." 'Sure' I replied. 'Now which court am I in?' I asked, he pointed me in the right direction then he was gone.

I sat at the back of the court until my name was called, then I made my way forward to the witness box, hear we go again I thought, all they had to do was to bring up what had happened at the Monk and I was fucked, nothing was mentioned, which I thought was a bit strange, but they did say they were having a recess which is highly unusual. They were gone for about twenty minutes, when they reappeared the chairman said "ok, licence granted Mr Kincaid you can leave the box," I said "thank you your worships" and promptly left the dock, I made my way along the corridor to the office of the licensing officer, the door was open, and as I tapped on it he looked up and said "come in Mr Kincaid and how did it all go?" 'Strange,' I said, 'it's the first time I have ever known the magistrates to have a recess in a licensing court, and to say I was a little bit concerned would be an understatement. "But there was no problem" he said, "I knew you would get your licence, I was out with the visiting magistrates a few days ago and we looked in at the Royal Oak, it was the evening time and a few of the undesirables were in, so I said to their worships, "we have just the right person coming in that will sort this lot out," then I mentioned your name, Johnny Kincaid the wrestling chappie, even they had heard of you."

Johnny Kincaid

By now I'm sitting up and taking notice, because there's something their not telling me about the pub I'm about to take over, ok we know it's a shit hole, but what's all this about the undesirables. 'What fucking undesirables?' I asked. "Hadn't Alex told you what kind of pub it is?" 'I thought a pub was a pub' I said. "Yes, but this pub is known for it's drugs, and the Brewery are on their last warning, if they don't get it sorted shortly, they will lose the pub for good." There's nothing like being pressured into something to get your nerve-ends tingling and your arse-hole twitching, what the hell had I let myself in for.

The afternoon of the day I took over we had the older customers in, (not nice to call them geriatrics) I was being looked over with the inquisitive eye, some gave me a smile, and some gave me the knowing nod, I could tell what they were thinking, yeh, I'm black, so I must be a junkie, into the ganja, weed, or even the white powder stuff. Not one welcomed me to the Royal Oak or enquired what intensions I had for the pub, just as well really, because I had no fucking idea myself,

I tried to be friendly and welcomed every one that came to the bar with a good afternoon sir/madam in my best West Indian voice, (just as a joke) which isn't very good at all, not many wanted to carry on a conversation with me, nobody enquired where I came from and only one asked why I wanted to run a shit hole like this, to be honest I was wondering that myself was my reply, but I do like a challenge, as he turned and walked away from the bar I heard him chuckling to himself, which didn't fill me with a whole lot of confidence. Between six or six thirty the bar was empting out of (geri) I mean older customers, and between seven and seven thirty the first of the so-called undesirables came walking through the door followed by about twelve others. I don't know if it was planned or it was a coincidence but they came walking in as if they were the mafia. If it wasn't so pathetic it would have been funny, I think this is where I was supposed to shit myself and show I was scared and worried, instead I said in my best cockney accent,' evening lads and what's your poison?' then I noticed one of the lads couldn't have been more than fifteen or sixteen years old, I pointed to him and said 'please don't ask for a beer.' One of the other lads piped up and said he was with him, "I don't care who he's with, he's not drinking in here, and if I catch him drinking, who ever brought him the drink will be barred as well, I'm telling you now so there won't be any misunderstanding later, he can sit in here with you and drink coke, and only coke, anything else will cause a problem and problems we can do with out, agreed?' I was looking at the big bloke leaning on the counter when I said that, and waited for his response, he gave a slight nod of his head, so I said again, 'ok lads what's your poison, and by the way my name's John and for the foreseeable future I'm the governor of this shit hole, if you want you can call me Gov.' With a big grin on my face I said 'I have been called a whole lot of other names, but make sure I'm in a good mood if you decide to call me them' which raised a chuckle out of most of them, at least I found out that most of them had a sense of humour, the rest of the

Johnny Kincaid

night passed without any concerns, even the young kid stuck to his coca cola, and no body lit up a joint, I didn't see any evidence of pill taking or white powder sniffing in the toilets so I would say my first day went without a hitch, more than I could say for the next day. It started of well in the afternoon with new faces in, old, but new faces to me, and more friendly than the ones I had in on the first day, at least these one's wanted to talk to me, even if it was just to be nosey. Later on we had a few of the lads in from the previous night, but tonight they seemed a bit more boisterous and loud, I let it go for a while and then went round by the pool table to collect some glasses and to see what was happening, I could smell it before I turned the corner, there were three of them that I could see smoking joints, two sitting and one playing pool, the one playing pool just looked up at me and carried on with his pool game with the joint sticking out of his mouth, when he had finished taking his shot I walked up to him and knocked him out, I turned on the other two and said, 'he got that for taking the piss, one for smoking a joint in here and two for smoking over the pool table, you can smoke shit until it comes out your ears for all I care but you do it out side, and if you give me a shout I will come out and join you, but you don't do it in here, because this is my living and I'm not about to lose my licence for any one of you, if it's pissing down with rain you can use my toilets to roll up but don't let me catch anyone smoking in there.' By this time the guy I hit was getting to his feet and he still had hold of the pool cue, "use it or put it down" I said "and if you decide to use it you had better be good, because if your not I guarantee I'll break your fucking arm in three places," I slowly walked towards him and he laid the cue on the table, I said, 'I'm not going to bar you this time, but don't ever take me for a twat again or take the piss.' When I turned back to the other two they had put their joints out, I smiled at them and said lets go out side and have a smoke shall we? 'I could do with mellowing out a bit.' We sat in the garden area for about an hour having a smoke and getting to know each other, I told them what I thought had happened, that they came in and tried it on to see what I would do, and if I did nothing, they would be running the pub again, I told them that's just not going to happen, and if they play ball with me I will play ball with them, we will have lock in's, but only when I want them not when they say, I also told them to tell the other lads what I had told them and if any of them fuck up they will be out straight away, and if any of them want to fight they do it out here in the garden not in the pub, I looked at matey and said "I'm the only one who can get away with that" and gave him a wink.

I started off slowly running pool tournaments to get the lads interested in their pub, I wouldn't allow betting on the table because that creates arguments, I've seen to many pool cues put across peoples heads. I charged everybody a pound entry fee, I said I would double the amount of the total entry fee, and the winner would take all, each game had an independent referee and his word was final, any arguments and the person involved would be barred, about fifteen entered for the first tournament so I had to fork out fifteen pounds as well but I had been running a meat raffle for the past two Sundays and had already cash in hand, I also arranged for a Karaoke on the Saturday night, I had a bar maid working for me (Anna) who asked if she would be allowed to sing, she was a big girl and I'm game for a laugh so I said ok, boy was I put in my place, this girl could sing, she sent shivers up and down my spine, what the fuck she was doing working behind my bar I don't know, but if that's what she chose to do, so be it. Anna has a brother Mark, a bloody good pool player, he used to stay behind and wait for Anna to finish then walk her home, I'm sure he only waited for her because he knew he would get another drink whilst he was waiting, anyway Mark use to go ferreting for rabbits and asked me if I liked rabbit, of course I did that's what we lived on when I was a kid, it was a cheap meal. One night Mark came into the pub with a carrier bag and asked if it was alright to go through to the kitchen, I nodded, finished pulling a pint for a customer and followed him through. "Here's your rabbits I promised" he said, "thanks" said I as I pulled one from the bag, 'it's still warm' I said, "it should be I only caught it half an hour a go." 'It's not been gutted" said I. "Fuck me do you want me to eat it for you as well, can't you do that?" said Mark. 'Can I fuck, I know how to cook the fucking thing but skinning and gutting it I've never done.' "Well there's only one way to learn and there's no time like the present," said he, "get me a sharp knife" which I did. "Now watch and learn, you start at the back end between his legs, you pull the skin up and slip the knife in, don't go to deep, you slip the knife right up the middle to his throat, then you do the same to his legs, now you start at his back legs, cut the paws off and pull the skin away from his legs, once that is done pull the skin all the way up to his front legs and do the same with them, then continue to the neck, now chop the head off with a bigger knife, now comes the part you really wont like, gutting it, this part is messy and smells, this is why you never go too deep at the beginning, because if you cut the gut bag you have the smell all the way through, so here we go, you cut along the gut cavity." 'Fucking hell' I said. "You get used to the smell after a while, but here comes the messy bit, you have to put your hand in and pull out all the guts, then push your fingers up towards the neck and you will feel a thin membrane, push your fingers through that and hook your fingers and pull back, you will bring back with you his heart and lungs, and that's it, just wash it through and it's all done, now you can do the other one while I'm here" he said, I must admit it wasn't that hard, and he was right, you do get used to the smell after a while.

One day after skinning and gutting a couple of rabbits, I had cut them up and put them in a saucepan with salt water, I had bagged the guts and fur and left them on the draining board, we had a meeting to go to in the afternoon, so we left some one to lock up, on our return I noticed the dogs were in the office, as it had been raining she had let the dogs in, but forgot to close the kitchen door, I saw a carrier bag over in one corner and straight away looked at the draining board, there was no carrier bag, slowly I walked over to it, expecting what I don't know, but there was nothing in it, I looked all over the place for the fur and heads, nothing did I find, I was just about to leave the kitchen when I noticed the saucepan was empty, yeh I mean empty salt water and all, those dogs were whining before I got to them, they knew they had done wrong. For the next few days I was checking their poo, because I was sure they would be shitting fur-balls.

I had left the Harts pub in Milton Keynes for about four months before I went back to see some of the old crew. I was having a drink with two or three of them when the loud mouth brother of the hard man came walking through the bar, he saw me, stopped and said "what the fuck you doing back here, we didn't like you when you were here," then he carried on walking through the door and out into the street. About fifteen minutes later he came back in and never said a word but on the way back from the toilet he stopped again and said, "are you still here why don't you fuck off" and with that walked back out into the street. Now the lad's were looking at me and I could read what they were thinking, I let him get away with it the first time am I going to let him get away with it a second time, I took another sip of my beer, placed the glass on the bar and said, 'I'll be back in a while,' as I stepped from the bar into the street loud mouth was just lighting a joint when I said to him, 'have you got a problem with me?' With that he jabbed his finger in to my chest and said, "yah you're my problem." When I got back to the bar I drank the rest of my beer and said, 'if he's not up in five minutes call an ambulance,' I said my good byes and never return to the Harts for five years.

Back at the Oak I approached a few of the older folk that used the pub to find out if they would be offended if I arranged an O.A.P.s Christmas party, some of them said it would never happen, and some of them were over the moon with the idea and suggested they make some mince pies, I told them that wouldn't be necessary as everything would be free and wouldn't cost them a penny.

I started to run a booze raffle on the Saturday night which was made up of Whisky, Barcardi, Gin, and four pints of beer, we started this in late May. I was selling the raffle tickets all though the week so we were taking a few bob and putting it in a savings account, by Christmas we had a fair amount saved and the O.A.P.s had a fair old treat. We were now getting about twenty odd players for the pool tournament on a Wednesday night, so I decided, what the pub could do with is a pool team. I picked out eleven players that I thought could be trusted to represent our pub in the league, it was harder than I thought, because half of them were barred from other pubs, we managed to get around that problem, I told the league I would be playing for the team and would be fully responsible for their behaviour, they said they would discuss it with the other landlords and would get back to me, the lads weren't to optimistic, they said they had tried to get back in a few times but always got a knock back, it had been four years since they last played in the league. The following week I had a nice letter from the chairman of the pool league saying congratulations the Royal Oak has been reinstated, but at the first sign of trouble the pub would be kicked out of the league without any warning and receive a life ban. Wednesday night half way through the pool tournament I called a halt to the proceedings, 'I have something to say, this morning I received a letter from the pool league, it read, a life ban, (pause) will be imposed on the Royal Oak (pause) if they are involved in any sort of trouble during the pool season, so congratulations we're back in the league and I want to see trophies coming this way after all the shit I've been through trying to get you back in.' You would have thought we had won the league already with the cheering and noise that was made, I thought, this would be a good night to have a lock in, and it was, the last one out left about three fifteen in the morning, a good night was had by all.

We ended up with a great bunch of customers, it was nice to see the old mixing with the young and there was none of them and us business, everybody had respect for each other, I even took a mixed party over to the Hamburg beer festival, it was so much fun seeing the youngsters looking after some of the olden's, and hearing some of the lads stories sitting in a bar late at night, one lad said he had taken this old couple down the Reeperbhan and every time they passed a sex shop the old dear would stop, have a good look and say "well I never," at one time he said, he was sure he heard the old man say under his breath "you did." How true this was I don't know but it was a good story at the time.

One day Alex came to me and said, "Johnny there's a pub in Hatfield I would like you to look at, it's much bigger than this and it's crying out for someone with your expert tees." 'So what your saying is it's another fucking rough pub' I said. "There's no drugs that I know of. 'So what are you saying, that it's a fighting pub?' "Its not even that, the manager that's in there now just can't handle them and to put it bluntly their taking the piss out of him." I told him I would take a look but if it's a fighting house he could keep it. "Fair do's" was his reply.

Later that week Jean and I took a short trip down to Hatfield. It was a Thursday night, normally Thursday nights were fairly quiet before the week-end rush, so we thought we could just walk in sit down and slowly look around at our leisure. Every thing went well until the manager came down, I had seen him at a couple of area meetings but never had much to do with him, as he came behind the bar he looked our way and recognized me. "Well if its not Johnny Kincaid he shouted" to draw attention to himself. "What are you doing down this neck of the woods?" he enquired in a loud voice. The mans a prick I thought to myself, he knows what I'm doing there, so why bring attention to himself, or maybe he don't. 'Just visiting' I said, with a smile on my face, 'nice place you got here' I said as I walked towards the counter, I didn't want him shouting across the bar at me all night. It's not bad, it's quiet to night but it gets busier over the weekend. What's with this guy, does he think I just walked into the job? How long have you been here then? I asked. About five months was his answer. As we were talking he pulled a pint for a customer, who took it and walked away, he shouted after him for the money, and the reply he got was yeh yeh I'll pay you in a minute. If I hadn't seen it with my own eyes I would never have believed it. 'I'm sorry my old son but if I were you I'd be straight round there taking the beer back, and the next time he came to the counter I would ask for his money first, he cant argue because he wouldn't get his beer until he'd paid.' "He's alright" he said, "he'll be over in a while and pay." Yeh, I thought to myself, and pigs might fly.

We stayed for about an hour, there was only one bar but it was very long and the counter was centralized, he said he had a kitchen out back but he didn't do a lot of food, there was also a very large garden with patio to the rear, and parking for around fifteen cars out front. I never enquired about the flat, I would get that information from Alex, but over all I would say it could be a very nice pub, I did notice one thing missing though, no pool table, I couldn't take a pub with no pool table I would get bored. Later that night after our pub had closed we sat down to discuss the pub we looked at, we agreed on most things so it was settled, we would take it, the only thing we were not looking forward to was packing up again, this would be the eighth time of moving pubs.

After everything was sorted with the area manager, it was time to let my staff and customers know what was happening, a day or so before we left Jean received the biggest bunch of flowers we had ever seen and I was visited by so many landlords of other pubs, wishing us all the best, the day we were leaving a lot of my customers took the day off work to see us off, it's a funny old game, you never know how much your appreciated until you leave, we got the biggest thank you card ever, which had been signed by everyone with their own little loving comments, even some of the villains said they were sorry to see us go, one of the messages read, "you were a hard bastard but fair," which meant a lot to me.

THE CAVENDISH ARMS

The day we stocked in at the Cavendish arms I found out that the out going manager had only been told a week before hand that he was going to be replaced, and he didn't know who was taking over until we arrived. He was a bit pissed off when he saw us because he went straight on the attack, swearing and saying we knew when we came down to see him that we had been offered the place. I told him I could understand him being pissed off, but I never knew if he had been told he was moving or not, and in any case it wasn't my place to tell him, so if he had to have a go, direct it towards the area manager not me, I didn't know if he was going to another pub or getting the elbow, so I didn't want to punch his lights out and add insult to injury.

I was looking around the pub and noticed a lot of things missing, like pictures off the wall, because they left marks where they were once hung, but the biggest mark was where an old railway clock once hung. I said to the out going manager 'what happened to all the pictures?' He said, "they were taken last night." 'Didn't you try to stop them" I asked. He said he was up stairs and when he came down the pub was bare and it was pointless asking who had taken what because no one would tell anyway. 'But your staff must have seen who took what.' "Sure they did but they're not going to get their faces punched in for grassing people up are they?" he said. 'No, but they could have told you, and in turn you could have told me, then I would have known who to look out for.' As it happened I befriended a guy later that day who had taken the clock, he had no qualms about telling me he had taken it, so I asked him if I could have it back. Only if I can have it again when you leave he said, if and when I leave you can take the tables and chairs as well for all I care, I would have said anything to get the clock back, it stood about four foot high by two and a half wide and it left a bloody big patch on the wall.

The following night there was a knock on my back door, when I opened it there it stood, the clock and a box with two pictures in, the bastard never told me he had them as well. "As promised, he said and I have spoken to some of the other lads and they may bring back their pictures, but that's up to them. I thanked him and asked him in for a drink. It later transpired that he was the boy friend of one of my bar staff.

A couple of days later one of my staff by the name of Sue came to me and said she was only helping out at the pub, and she would stay for another couple of weeks until I was settled, then she would go back to her own job, working the bar in another pub called the Harrier, or commonly known as, (the Hill Top). I noticed over the next couple of weeks that Sue had the respect of all the customers, and a lot of the Hill Top lads had started to drink here, she was a good laugh and sometimes an air head, like the time I was trying to put her through her N.V.Q, she would forget to take a book home then she would forget to bring in the paper work, where it should have taken a month it took three but we finally got her through it and there was another time she phoned to say she couldn't make it in because she had had an accident, she had electrocuted herself, she was wall paper stripping at her mums house when the wall paper stripper slipped and went behind the light switch, a bolt of electricity shot up her arm and knocked her off her chair, I had visions of her ginger (sorry strawberry blond) hair standing up on end and the shocked (no pun meant) look on her face. I couldn't stop laughing, I told her to come in when she felt better, and I didn't want to hear any more shocking news. I was working in the cellar this particular day cleaning the pipes, when Sue came in to get some ice from the machine. Good morning she said. Good morning said I. After she had filled the ice bucket she turned and left, about fifteen minutes later when I had finished what I had to do I tried to leave the cellar but found the door wouldn't open. I pulled it and pushed it but it wouldn't budge, I called Sue for about five minutes at the top of my voice, but did she hear me, did she hell, I banged on the roof with the scrubbing broom, but still she never heard me, there's only one way out I thought to myself, through the beer hatch, that's where they drop the kegs down the cellar from the street. I preceded to climb the steep stairs to the metal doors that covered the hatch, luckily I had the keys on me to the cellar so I had no difficulty in unlocking and unbolting the flap doors, the only trouble I had was lifting the fucking things, as they were made of heavy metal, by the time I got out I was sweating buckets. As I walked into the pub through the front doors, Sue looked up and said, "I never saw you come up from the cellar" of course you fucking didn't, because I have just come up through the fucking flaps," with that Sue put her hand to her mouth, and I heard her say under her breath "oh shit." 'And what's the oh shit for?' I asked. "I think I put the bolt across the door after getting the ice." ' You dozy mare, what did you do that for?" "Habit she said, I always bolt the door after I leave, that's what you've always told us to do." 'But you saw me in there.' "I know, but its Monday morning, and I'm never with it on a Monday morning." From then on, if ever I was in the cellar and Sue came down, I made sure we left together, once bitten twice shy, as the saying goes. I asked Sue if she would like to run her own pub some day, she said she didn't know, so I started to teach her the bookwork, and the ins and outs of running a pub. Months later I asked her if she thought she could handle doing a holiday relief for me, I told her that there were plenty of managers around that would help her if she ever got stuck, she agreed to give it a go, and it was a life changing decision. After I left the Cavendish it had a few different managers. One day I had a telephone call from my old area manager, (Robin Tidd,) asking if I knew of anyone that would like to take over the Cavendish. I asked him casually if Sue Milla was still there, he assured me she was. Then give her a chance, said I. But she's a woman, do you think she could handle and control all the rough ones? I said, 'she has more respect than any manager you have ever had in their, and that includes me.' Sue got her chance, and has never looked back; she now runs her own pub (The Vine) in Spalding Lincolnshire. Her two weeks stay with me turned into two and a half years, and she was the best barmaid (bar-person) I ever employed.

MY HIP REPLACEMENT

It was while I was at the Cavendish Arms that I went into hospital to have my hip operation. Over the last year it slowly got worse, I couldn't sit for very long before it gave me pain and when I went to bed the slightest movement would wake me up, I couldn't turn in bed without waking. One morning I said, 'enough is enough.' I was walking along the corridor to the toilet holding on to both side walls in excruciating pain, I made my mind up there and then that I was going to have the op, yes I was frightened but I couldn't take this pain any more. Years before hand I was due in to have the hip replaced but I bottled out after seeing the operation on television.

(We were at Kincaid's at the time). "Have a look at this" said Jean one afternoon after we had closed the pub. 'What is it? I asked as I was making a cup of coffee. "Its Jimmy's" said Jean, you know the hospital programme, there're showing a hip operation." I was in my armchair double quick, I had left the coffee where it stood, and my eyes were fixed to the TV screen. I thought I was coping quite well until he took the mallet and started banging in this long silver pin, with every bang I was slipping further and further down in my seat and I said, 'do you think there're going to do that to me? They've got more chance of farting in a space suite.'

Seven years after making that comment and suffering years of pain, I was about to eat my words. After phoning my consultant Mr Gunn who had told me many years before that if I didn't stop or slow down in the wrestling business he would be putting a plastic hip in me within eight or nine years, he was right, because here I was seven years on and in total pain. He made arrangements to have me admitted on Friday the 4th of June, I was horrified, not on the 4th of June, its my birthday and I want to do the twist for the last time. He wasn't known for his sense of humour but for some reason he found that funny and changed the date to the 6th, which was fine by me because I called it My D-Day. The day of the operation a friend of mine (Terry) drove me to the hospital in Milton Keynes. We were in my room when a nurse came in to give me the procedure of events that was about to happen, and to ask me some personal questions. She said, "do you mind talking in front of your friend or would you prefer him to leave?" I said 'I'm easy with the situation.' During our conversation she told me I would have to wear stockings for a while after the operation. Terry's head nearly done a complete turn just like Chuckys and he had this god-awful smirk on his face. I said to the nurse 'you shouldn't have said that in front of him, now I'm really in for some shit.' Just as she was finishing the anaesthetist came in to tell me that I would be going down shortly, and what she was going to do to me, she also asked if I was worried. 'Me worried, no, petrified, yes." "Would you like a pre-med?" she asked. 'Lets put it this way, if you don't give me one, I will be off the trolley and legging it down the corridor never to be seen again.' It was the first time she smiled since walking into the room.

About half an hour later the nurse came in and gave me a tiny tablet to take. 'What's this for?" I asked. "It's your pre-med" she replied. I was shocked, I had visions of a bloody great needle being shoved up my arse, quarter of an hour later this guy came in and started messing around with my bed, then he preceded to push it out of the door and along the hall way, it was a funny sensation, it felt like I was floating, I must have fell a sleep because when I opened my eyes there was this guy standing at my head looking down at me, I asked him if it was usual to want a pee. "Do you want to" he asked, 'yes' said I. "You can't get of the bed, just stay there and I will be straight back." He was true to his word he came back holding a cardboard urinal, he sat me up and held me while I had the longest pee I've ever had, when I had finished he started to laugh and said "thank god you got rid of all that, other wise you would have pissed over everybody around the table." I don't know where it all came from because I hadn't had a drink since ten o'clock the previous night, shortly after I was pushed through some doors where the anaesthetist greeted me with "hello John, are you feeling relaxed now, I'm just going to give you a little injection and I want you to count back wards from ten." To tell you the truth I don't even remember saying ten, what I do remember is opening my eyes and seeing a bag of white fluid hanging up to my left, then turning my head to the right I saw a bag of red fluid, that's all I remember, I must have gone back to sleep because I was woken with the phone ringing, "hello" I said. It was my daughter Tasha, she did most of the talking because as she told me later I was incoherent, I understood every word she said but my speech was coming out all gobble-de-gook, it sounded alright to me.

All through this, there was one thing I noticed, there was no pain, I lifted the sheet to look at my thigh, there was a long blue plaster and two tubes protruding from my leg, but there was no pain. I must have nodded of again because when I came around Mr Gunn (my surgeon) was standing by the side of my bed. "Well Mr Kincaid you bleed very well" he said, " when we had finished it looked like we had just come out of an abattoir, we had to put six units in you." I remember asking him how many units do we have, "eight" was his reply, and then he was gone.

My recuperation in hospital went well, in total I was in there for five days. I decided to go back to my house for a week or so instead of going straight back to the pub.

My best mate Phil who does my pub relief's for me, picked me up from hospital and dropped me of home. Jean and Tasha met me at the door and helped me in, Phil had to get back to the pub as it was a Friday and he had left his wife alone.

I had made my way into the kitchen on my crutches when Tasha asked me if I wanted anything to eat, it was lunch time but I didn't fancy anything to heavy, 'have you got any Rice Krispies? I asked. While Tasha went to prepare the Rice Krispies Jean got a couple of cushions to put on the kitchen chair as I wasn't allowed to sit low, I made myself comfortable with my dodgy left leg sticking out straight and preceded to eat my Krispies. I managed to eat two spoonfuls and the third one hit the ceiling, I screamed with the pain that ran from my ankle to my head, I think Jean and Tasha screamed with me, I jumped up quick and grabbed my sticks, 'it's ok' I said, 'it's a muscle spasm.' Well that's what I thought it was until I looked down at my foot which wasn't where it should have been, when I stuck my foot out in front of me I was resting on my heel instead of my foot being flat on the floor, the consequences were, when I relaxed and my foot turned out, it took my hip out as well, and because I jumped up quick it came completely out of the socket and my foot turned completely to the side (not a pretty sight). I have never touched Rice Krispies since, you can keep the snap crackle and pain. In total my hip dislocated itself six times in five weeks and the funniest time was when it came out for the fourth time, don't get me wrong there's nothing funny about the pain, just the episode that followed.

I was in bed with Jean, (no, we hadn't been getting up to any funny business.)

I sat bolt up right in bed, the clock was showing on the dressing table that it was seven fifteen in the morning; something wasn't quite right with my leg. I woke Jean and told her to phone an ambulance. "Why?" she asked. 'Because my hip is coming out.' "Your paranoid" she replied. 'And I have every right to be, but it feels like it's coming out so will you phone for a fucking ambulance or not?' With that she jumped out of bed, and that's all it took, the movement of the mattress did the rest, and I was back in excruciating pain, it took less than fifteen minutes for the ambulance to arrive, and as the paramedics came though the door I was screaming at them to give me some pain relief shit, I don't remember them saying a word to me just injecting a double bang of pain killer into my arm, it started to work within three or four minutes, it didn't take the pain completely away but it certainly took the edge off it.

What happened next could have been written as a comedy script. The paramedics were discussing between themselves, which would be the best way to get me out. Let me put you in the picture, outside the bedroom was a corridor, not a very wide corridor. At the end of the corridor was a very steep stairway, at the bottom of the stairway was a very large window and to the right of the window was the door leading to the back entrance where the ambulance was, now there was no way they could use a traditional stretcher because it would have been impossible to turn it in or out of the bedroom, so they came up with the idea of using a blow up airbed which they had in the ambulance, so far so good, except when they tried to blow it up they found it had a puncture, this is when one of them took a good look at me and asked how heavy I was. 'Seventeen and a half to eighteen stone' I replied. "We need another ambulance" he said, I started to laugh uncontrollably, they looked at me as if I had lost it. 'Another ambulance' I said, 'What you going to do, cut me in fucking half.' Now they could see the funny side of what had been said, then one of them explained, it would take more than the two of them to carry me down the stairs, and they should have a blow up bed on board, hopefully without a puncture. The second ambulance arrived within ten minutes of the call, the two paramedics, one a woman, brought in with them the air-bed, which they preceded to blow up, except it wasn't going up. We were all thinking the same thing, not another bloody puncture, until Jean noticed the bung was out at the end, whoever let it down last never put the bung back in. After the bed was fully blown they manoeuvred me on to it and strapped me down across the arms, waist and ankles, it wasn't until they had bent me around the doorframe that I said, 'am I going down the stairs headfirst? "Why's that" one asked, 'because the stairs are behind you' I said. "Stand him up and turn him around" another said, so up on end I went, I was strapped in so well I never slipped an inch, but I had the fright of my life when they got me to the top of the stairs, in front of me, on her own was the woman paramedic. Houdini would have been proud of me; I escaped from the strapping around my arms and held on to the edge of the wall. "What are you doing?" asked one of them. 'Get another person in front" I said. "You will be ok" came the reply. 'Not if any of you slip and lets me go I won't, I would plough straight over her and out the fucking window so get another person in front as well." I suppose they could see my point as it would have been very difficult for three of them to hold one end of the bed on a narrow stairway, as one of them climbed over me and stepped on to the air bed it tipped to one side, I let out an almighty scream followed by a torrent of abuse, which I did apologise for a while later, anyway at the bottom of the stairs there was no room to manoeuvre me round so they had to lift me over the banisters, in all it took over an hour to get me into the ambulance and about fifteen minutes to get me to the Q.E.2 hospital in Welwyn Garden City. The following day my mate Phil who was doing my relief came to see me. I apologised profusely for kicking up so much rumpus and disturbing his sleep the previous morning, in fact I think I went over the top with the apologises and do you know what he said, "when I got up I said to mum, (that's what he calls Jean) did John have a good nights sleep? When she told him I was back In hospital he couldn't believe it, he never heard a bloody thing, yet when the dogs bark because the cleaner is banging on the window to be let in, he's out of bed like a shot, so there you have it, he takes more notice of the fucking dogs than of me, but we're still the best of friends.

I arranged a Beer Fest trip to Hamburg one October and to tell you the truth I could have filled the entire coach with my pub alone, but then all the heavy drinkers would have been with me in Hamburg and my profit margin in the pub would have been way down, so I always made it a rule never to take more than fifteen people at any one time. The coach company phoned to say they would be picking us up between eleven and eleven thirty Sunday morning, so I made sure all my lads were at the pub by ten thirty, there's always one or two that have to make a late entrance, this way we wont have to sit around waiting for them. The coach arrived about Eleven o'clock and the coach driver informed me that we were the last to be picked up, some of the lads on the coach asked if they could use the toilets and a few asked if they could have a beer, I said it's up to the driver, if he thinks we have time I don't mind serving you, the driver gave them half hour. I'm glad Sue walked through the door when she did, as I had never worked so hard in such a short time. I said sorry to Sue as we were leaving, as I left her with all the washing up to do.

There was no trouble on the trip, and everybody enjoyed them selves, in fact they wanted me to arrange another trip as soon as possible, which of course I did for the end of January and all this was done before we got back to the pub, and there were guys from another pub in St Albans that wanted to come in on the next trip in January. When we arrived back, Sue and Jean had just closed up for the afternoon, the look on Sue's face was a picture, you could tell what was going through her head, (no not again), but money is money, and you have to take it when you can, and there was no time like the present. Some of the lads had to go all the way back to Manchester and was unlikely to get another beer stop. By the time all the other pubs had been dropped off in various parts of the country they would probably get back to their own pub after closing time, Sue has never let me forget that one.

It was a Friday night when I drove down to Milton Keynes to pick up Phil. Jean and I were leaving for Turkey the following morning and Phil was doing our relief. As we left Phil's place he asked if I had any fags on me. 'I smoked the last one just before I arrived, we could stop and buy a packet" I said. The London Pride pub was just around the corner. 'We might as well have a beer while we're here.' "Any excuse for a Gin and Tonic" Phil said. 'Too right mate' was my answer. I had the shock of my life on entering the pub, there couldn't have been more than sixteen people in the main bar, and this was on a Friday night. I remember this pub always being packed even in the weekdays. 'What the hell's happened to this place?' I enquired of Phil. "Don't know mate, I stopped using the Pride about a year ago." I ordered a Gin and Tonic and was informed they only did Tonic in a can, 'Tonic is Tonic I replied, be it in a bottle or a can, just as long as my gin comes from a bottle I'll be happy.' Phil ordered a pint of Guinness and was told they haven't any. "A pub with out Guinness you are joking of course," he said. "No, but we have Guinness in a can" the bar maid said, "no thanks" said Phil, "give me a Scotch, I presume you do Whiskey?" he said in a very sarcastic way. Someone tapped me on the shoulder and as I turned I came face to face with one of my old customers from the Bow Bells. "Hello Shaky" I said, (his real Name was Liam) he was called Shaky because until he has had about four or five pints of Guinness his hands won't stop shaking. "Are you taking over?" he asked. 'Taking what over?' I enquired. "This place, it's up for grabs, it has been for the last ten months, take it John and I'm sure all the old customers would come back." Before Phil and I had finished our drinks at least another twelve people had asked me the same question, am I taking the Pride?, On the way back to the Cavendish, Phil said, "well, are you?," 'It's a thought,

I will have to think about that one. Now the old brain was ticking away, and for the next two weeks in Turkey I did nothing but think about the Pride. Would it be a good move moving back onto the Lakes Estate?

Holiday over, I set about finding out more about the London Pride. I got in touch with the Brewery to find out the asking price but before I went to far I had to find out if I could get my licence back in Milton Keynes, the licensing officer had changed, there was a new lady in charge by the name of Helen. I phoned her to make an appointment, and when she answered the phone she said, "hello John, its been a long time, you probably won't remember me but I used to be on the beat when you had 'Kincaid's,' I came in a few times with the sergeant, you know, when he had his coffee with a Woods Rum in it?" Now I could put a face to the voice. "What can I do for you John?" she asked. "I would rather talk to you face to face if you don't mind Helen, could I make an appointment to see you some time next week?" "I'm free next Wednesday morning, can you make it then?" she asked. 'I'll be there' I said, we made a time and she rang off, I had to wait nearly a week before our meeting and I was trying to think of all the reasons why they wouldn't give me my licence back, do you know, I couldn't think of one, I had only six weeks to go before my five years of being out of Milton Keynes was up, five years of being away from my family and friends. The day of the meeting Helen greeted me like a long lost friend, she wanted to know what I had been doing in the last five years, I told her of the two pubs I had run, one being a druggie pub that I cleaned up and turned into a family pub, the other I turned into a sporting pub, darts, pool, and I sponsored the football team that came second in the league that year, but what I really want to know is there any chance of me getting my licence back in Milton Keynes? "Well John" she said, I thought, here it comes. "You shouldn't have left in the first place" she said. 'Don't piss me about, what do you mean by that?' I asked. "Myself and four other officers said to the new inspector, leave Mr Kincaid's licence alone, he has run a number of heavy pubs in the area, and we have never had any trouble from them, and I suppose because he was new, he wanted to prove he was the boss, and make an example of you, anyway, you must have served your five years exemption by now, so you can come back any time you like, but I don't know of any managed houses going." 'Its not a managed house I'm looking at, it's a tenancy' I said. "Oh, which one?" she asked. 'The London Pride I replied. (quote) Her exact words were, "are you fucking mad?"

Naturally I wanted to know why she thought I was mad. "The Pride is having its windows put in every week." 'Any names in the frame' I enquired. "Only one," she said. When she told me I laughed, 'that wont be a problem I ensured her, he's like a brother to me, I go on the occasional holiday with his parents.' our meeting ended and Helen ensured me she and her office would not oppose my application for a liquor licence, I left that police station floating on air and in the famous words of Paul Newman in The Colour of Money, I was thinking to myself ------I'M BACK.

I had another three Months at the Cavendish before all the legal paper work had gone through, all the legal shit, signing of this and signing of that between my solicitor and the company briefs. My solicitor actually told me to walk away from it, but me being a stubborn bastard thought I knew best so I signed a ten-year lease on the property. My solicitor told me not to sign the final contract until the company had done the work that they verbally agreed to do. I was glad that I took his advise on that occasion.

My last few weeks at the Cavendish was like a night mare, my punters got a petition up with well over a thousand names on it, they sent it to our area manager, and he in turn came down to see us about thinking over our intentions of leaving. He could understand our reasons for wanting to get back to Milton Keynes but said, 'you have such a good name in the area that obviously the community don't want to see you leave and a lot of the names on the petition were from punters from other pubs, now that shows how much respect they have for you.' He nearly had me in tears; he was making me think I was the next best thing to sliced bread. Every day up until our leaving party we had people asking us to reconsider and stay. I held our leaving party on the Sunday. A day before we left on the Monday, I wanted to go out with a bang. Friday and Saturdays were always good. I wanted to see how many would turn up knowing they had work the next day. It was madness; I took more money than I did on Friday and Saturday put together, it was a night I will never forget, the well-wishers, the flowers, and the plaque that was presented to me from the football team with the words, 'Simply the Best Governor.' (They knew my favourite singer was Tina Turner).

The last person left the pub that night about twelve fifteen, the police came in around eleven thirty and wanted to know why the pub wasn't cleared, and I explained it was my last night and I had a going away party. They could see I was not serving any more drinks as the tills were out and I told them, as the lad's finish their drinks I'm taking their glasses and ushering them out. I'm not stupid enough to try and take their glasses when there's beer in them, not unless I want a fight on my hands, this way they finish their drinks, say their good bye's and leave happily. They said they could see the sense in that, they also said they were sorry to see me go and wished me all the best in my new pub, I thanked them and they left, I think they were rather relieved that they didn't have to remove any of the heavy Hill Top boy's that were still hanging around.

The next day as we were loading a few more items onto the removal wagon, I was beginning to have my doubts about going. Jean kept on asking what was wrong, and I kept on saying nothing, but she knew me better than I knew myself. "Your thinking, have you fucked up leaving this place? Well, the only way we'll know that is if we don't make a go of it at the Pride, because it won't be the brewery's money that we'll be losing, it will be ours." 'I know that, that's what I'm frightened of.' "Well stop worrying and think positive. You have never fucked up yet and have always made money for every company we've worked for so what makes you think your going to mess up now?" She was right of course; I should have taken my own advice,

Because I always say, never worry until you have something to worry about, because it may never happen.

Jean stayed at the Cavendish for another three weeks until they got a company relief in. I left one of the dogs with her and took the other with me, I didn't know if the Pride was alarmed as I had a falling out with the previous governor over it, the foolish man was asking a thousand pound for it, I said 'ok, but I will get my man to check it out first just to make sure it's working ok.' "Tell him to phone me first or he won't get in," he said. I thought what a strange request but I went along with his wishes. My friend went to check the alarm system but before he even looked at it the governor said he wanted a thousand pound. "Ok mate but I haven't even looked at it yet." "Yeh, but I want a thousand pound for it," the governor said again. My friend has a bit of a short fuse and it's a wonder he hadn't smacked him in the mouth by now. My friend asked again nicely if he could look at the alarm, the foolish man said, "you can look as much as you like but it doesn't matter what you say, I still want a thousand pound for it." How my friend kept his hands of him I don't know, he's a very lucky man, but he phoned me straight away to tell me what had happened, in turn I phoned the governor and told him to stick the fucking alarm system up his arse because he won't be getting a penny out of me for it. I still believe to this day that he never brought it in the first place, because I'm sure it was in there before he moved in, to cut a long story short he sold it to the brewery for eight hundred pounds and I brought it from the brewery for the same. Eventually when my friend did get around to checking it out, he said the same system now would cost around fourteen hundred pounds, so the stupid twat done himself out of two hundred quid. That's life!

THE LONDON PRIDE

I tried to engage the services of Giant Haystacks to open the London Pride for me but his contract for the States had already come through and he was leaving for America two days before my opening, so I managed to get my old mate big Pat Roach of Auf Wirdersehen Pet fame to do the honours. On the night of the opening my pub was packed to the rafters, they were all waiting for big Pat to arrive when someone said, "Is that him John?" I saw a body walk past the window, no head just a body. 'I have a feeling it could be' I said and as he came through the door I heard someone say "fuck me I never realized he was that big." Pat was only six foot four tall but had the presence of a man much taller, Pat had brought some out-takes of Auf Wirdersehen Pet down with him so I played them on the big screen, afterwards when Pat made a speech in his native Brommie accent somebody shouted "how comes you don't talk like Bomber? as quick as a flash Pat said in a Cornish accent "Bomber wouldn't like that Bomber wouldn't".

Haystacks tour of America was cut short as he was taken ill, and was taken into hospital where they discovered he had stomach cancer; which eventually took his life.

Although Martin was portrayed as a villain in the ring, he was in fact a gentleman with a heart as big as his body, he would help anybody at any time, it was amazing to see how far people had travelled to be at the big mans funeral, there were wrestlers from Scotland and Wales and all over England, he got one hell of a send off, God bless you Martin, they didn't come any bigger than you. My first day in the Pride, I had let the bar-maid in and she opened the bar while I was helping unload the removal van, we had nearly finished when I heard this loud mouth person in the bar, I poked my head around the corner and saw this six footer

Standing there being rather gobbie. I thought to myself I'm not going to like him, and I had the feeling we were going to fall out. All that morning I never went behind the bar once, I concentrated on getting all the right things placed in the right rooms, other wise I would really be In the shit when Jean gets here, there was still a fair amount to come up from the Cavendish like our double bed, the three piece suite, units, wardrobes etc. By the time we had carried the boxes up stairs and sorted them it was three o'clock and Eileen the bar maid had closed the doors, she shouted up that she was off and would see me at seven o'clock. I thanked her and said 'ok'. I was a bit knackered myself so I thought I would go across to the Chinese and get something to eat then have a bath, have a short kip, and then I would be ready for the evening session, it sounded good to me, if only it had worked out that way. The Chinese meal was lovely as always, they had been there a long time and was very popular. When I had finished my meal I ran a bath, I had a portable T.V so I sat down to watch it while the bath filled, I gave it about ten minutes then went to check on the bath water, I put my hand in the water and nearly came away with no skin on it, I ran the hot and cold together, but for some reason the cold water had stopped coming through, I had no idea why so I phoned my brother in-law Tony who is a jack of all trades, he assured me he would be over first thing in the morning, and true to his word he was. It wasn't until I put the phone down on Tony that I noticed there was no bulb in the light socket, in fact, there were no bulbs in any of the light sockets except the one in the lounge, the cheeky bastard had taken them all. I phoned my daughter Tasha and told her I was on my way over to use the bath, in those days she was a girl of very few words, all I got was, "ok dad." Later I gave her a job in the pub and created a monster, a nice monster, but that's another story that comes later.

When Tony arrived he asked where the stopcock was, now that's a silly question to be ask me, (I've never asked my cock to stop, ever) I didn't have the foggiest idea. It took him about five minutes to find it, he said, "their never where you expect them to be." After turning it off, he opened all the taps in the flat until they ran dry, then he turned all the taps off and opened the stop cock again, one by one he turned on a tap, "no water" he said. 'I can see that' was my answer. "It has to be your water tank." 'Where's that' said I. "In your loft I imagine, have you got any ladders here?" he asked. I just laughed and shook my head. "It will have to be your shoulders then." He sat on my shoulders and started to laugh, 'if you fart, I'll drop you straight on your head," I said. First one foot then the other and he was standing on my shoulders, in the next instant he was through the hatch. I heard him moving around up there and then all of a sudden this bloody wet thing hit me on the head. "That" he said, "Was wedged in and blocking the feed pipe." It wasn't until I had a good look at it that I noticed it was a sock. 'How the fuck did that get up there? "It had to be put there, because there was a cover over the tank, Tony said." 'The slimy no good bastard, if ever I see him again I'll ram this fucking sock down his fucking throat.' My fury grew over the next few days. The next thing I noticed was, there was no toilet seat in the loo he had taken that as well, so every time I wanted to go for a pony, I had to use the staff room down stairs. Later that evening somebody asked if they could have the T.V on. 'No problem' I said, how wrong could I be, every channel showed snow, the Ariel was in so why was it showing snow? I followed the ariel cable through the wall to the electric cupboard and what did I find, the cable had been cut, not just cut, but about two foot cut out of it, so the two ends didn't meet, he was one vindictive twat. I later found out that most of his customers had chinned him at some time or another and it didn't take a brain surgeon to understand why.

The following day I put a notice on the window stating that we were closing for three days. There was a number of reasons for this, (one) we hardly had any beer left, (two) fuck knows when the pipes were last cleaned, you couldn't see through the Lager, (three) after trying to clean the pipes specially the ones in the games room, I had gone through them at least three times and the cleaning fluid was still coming out like black molasses. It came to light that he hadn't opened the games room bar for at least a year and when he closed it he just left the beer in the pipes instead of cleaning them out and leaving water in them. I had to phone beer services to come and replace all the pipes, the ones in the lounge wasn't all that clever either, and (four) the whole pub needed a fucking good clean, it really was a shit hole. I was beginning to think I should have listened to my solicitor after all, that's why you employ them, for their expertise and advice, unless you're a stubborn bastard like me. I had listened to all his arguments against taking the pub, and there were a lot, and still I said I think I can do something with it, basically the only advice I took was not to sign the full lease contract until all the work that he had marked out was done, like the big plated window that was broken in the Off licence and boarded up, and the replacement of floor tiles in the roof garden, because rain was leaking through into the games room, a couple of window frames were also letting in rain water, there was also damp patches in the flat that needed to be sorted, other than that I thought everything else was fairly ok, how wrong I was.

I asked Eileen if she and her husband Boh would like to come in and do the cleaning for me while we were closed for the three days, and if they found anything that was missing to write it down or replace it and give me the bill. Light bulbs, toilet seats, (four) and toilet utensils, that's all they could come up with, and after the three days the place sparkled and had a refreshing smell to it. The Dray came at eight thirty Friday morning with the biggest delivery they had ever dropped in over a year at the Pride. When they had finished I asked them in for a drink, the best way to find out what is happening in the brewery or other pubs in your area is to ask a drayman, they know everything and I mean that in the nicest way.

It was eleven o'clock opening time and Eileen had just opened the doors, when through the door came the loud mouth fella that I saw on the first day. "Morning" he said, in a much quieter voice, 'Morning' said I. "Well he's gone then, I don't suppose he left my wheel ramps out anywhere did he" he asked. 'What wheel ramps are they?' said I. "I did some work on his car which I haven't been paid for and I left my wheel ramps here as well." 'You can have a look in the garage if you like, but I cant say I have seen them.' He had a look around the garage but couldn't find them, then he asked if he had left a forwarding address, I can honestly say a definite no to that question. After talking to this guy for about half an hour I was beginning to like him, he was easy to talk to and you felt comfortable in his company, first impressions are not always lasting impressions, his name is Dave and he will be cropping up again later on. Over the next few days most of my old Bow Bell customers had been in to see me and welcomed me home, it was nice to feel wanted straight off and not to have people wanting to fight you, in fact one lad came in and said "your Johnny Kincaid aren't you?" 'Yes son' I am. "My old man said if I use this pub not to fuck up, because if I do there's a chance you will come round my house and sort me out, apparently that's what you did to my dad." 'Is your dads name Alex?' I asked. He nodded. 'Tell him he has a good memory but I have mellowed in my old age, and it would be nice to see him again.' With a smile he turned and left, I don't think I ever had trouble from that boy.

Over the next few days a couple of girls I knew from the Bow Bells and Kincaid's came round to see me, we won't go into detail but the expression, 'while the cats away the mice will play' comes to mind, well I was highly sexed in those days and I had been away from the wife for over a week, that's no excuse I hear you say to yourself, but I was a sex addict and couldn't help myself, sure there were places to go to get cured but why stop something you enjoy, as long as nobody gets hurt you tell yourself, but then you would, an addict is an addict and will always find an excuse or a reason to carry on doing what he's doing even if it does hurt somebody. I sincerely apologise to the one person I must have hurt a lot, I never meant to hurt her, I was just plain selfish and irresponsible.

My old Scottish friends the two John's, Morrison & Branter came into see me, and it seemed we took up where we had left off, having a great laugh and joke. The place was getting busy and Eileen and I were rushed of our feet, she said she had never seen it that busy, although I had back in the old days. I was thankful when an old barmaid of mine walked through the door.

In a broad Irish accent she shouted, "I knew there could only be one fucking Kincaid running a pub on the Lakes Estate, welcome home me darling. 'Thanks Ann' I said, 'now do me a favour and get your arse behind here and give us a hand. I didn't have to ask her twice, she came straight behind and started abusing the customers, that was the great thing with Ann, she could really abuse you and you wouldn't take offence, you would just end up laughing your bollocks off at the way she did it. At the end of the session I asked Ann if it was like old times being back behind the bar with me, "Be Jesus it was" was her answer. Well do you want the job or don't you?' I asked her. "I didn't know there was a job going." 'There is and it's yours if you want it.' "I'll take it," she said leaning across the bar and giving me a big wet kiss. There was never anything between Ann and I but I bet a lot of people thought there was because of the way we carried on.

There was less than a week to go before Jean would be joining me, I had cleaned the flat as much as I could with the help of my daughter Tasha. I was going over to my house most days because Tasha was doing my washing, and I was taking a shower there, plus I was trying to talk her into working for me.

It was a night just before Jean arrived that the electrics went for the first time throwing the pub into total darkness, luckily there was a guy in the pub that knew something about electrics, because I know sod all, and by the time I had got somebody out from the electricity board the night would have gone and I would have had to close, anyway this guy became a life saver, any little thing that went wrong I could call him up and he would be straight out, his name was also Dave, so I nicked named him (D.I.Y. Dave). Dave and I were talking one day and he mentioned something about when he was in the army in Germany, naturally I started to take notice because Germany was like my second home, I loved the place, I worked in most of the big City's and a hell of a lot of the smaller towns. When Dave had finished talking I asked him if he would like to go back for a long weekend. "Where" he asked. 'Too the Hamburg Beer Festival' I replied, or we could fly out before that and stay in a friends Hotel in the Reeperbhan.' "Sounds good to me but I will have to get the ok from the wife." 'With respect Dave, so will I' I said. "What about friends, can I bring a friend? he asked." 'No more than two, six in a group is a comfortable number when flying out and I have two people that I want to ask.' "That's fine, I'll be in touch" he said and he was. A few days later, he let me have the two names of his travelling companions, Roy & Jeff. Roy ran a pub in Luton and was an ex Boxer, Jeff was a boiler engineer, two nicer guys you could never wish to meet. My two companions were Gary & Dave, Gary was a millionaire who had his own computer company, and Dave was the first person I spoke to in the pub. Although Gary's a millionaire he's a down to earth kind of person and Dave turned out to be a real genuine kind of guy. It wasn't until I met D.I Y' Daves friend Roy, who was really a friend of Jeff's, that I recognized him from another pub he had way back in the Eighties, I remembered taking a pool team over to his place and kicking their arse. He told me we were the first team to beat them at home that season, and he brought my team a round of drinks.

Jeff was definitely a ladies man, good looking with jet black hair, a nice lean body, he didn't have to pull the birds they pulled him, he was like a magnet to them, but the time that made Jean and I laugh the most is when he told us he was fast approaching forty, he literally had tears in his eyes, I kid you not. He seemed petrified of reaching that age, I'm sure he thought he would get a beer belly and his cock would shrink, his balls would sag and his arse would get wrinkly, it took a lot to convince him it didn't happen over night but there were a lot of old codgers in and someone said, one day you will look just like them, how he held back the tears I don't know.

Gary was a self-made millionaire. He started his computer business working from home, and then gradually expanded to a bloody big complex near the city. He liked his trimmings, but then who wouldn't with his money, he had his nice big house, his nice car (A Porche) and a Rolex which we threatened to take off him and throw in the river Elbe if he ever said, "the time on my Rolex watch is," ever again, but we will come to that a bit later. Gary on the hole was a great guy, he was down to earth with a good sense of humour.

Big Dave or Dave the post as I will call him (because he became a postman a little while later) had a dry sense of humour, but was fun to be with, so in all we had a good team to travel with. When Jean arrived I think she was pleasantly surprised with the cleanness of the place but after putting all her personals away she came into the lounge and said, "This place needs decorating." I expected her to say something like that as every pub we had except for two she would end up decorating the lounge, I'm not knocking her as she was a bloody good decorator but I think it was more a woman thing. It wasn't badly decorated; in fact it looked pretty good, me. I'll live anywhere as long as its clean, but no not her, she said, "its now my home and I want it the way I want it, not the way somebody else had it," so within a week or two we had a nice new lounge.

Jean and I had been at the Pride for about a month when the main cellar-cooling generator packed up. I phoned my area manager straight away. "What do you want me to do about it John?" he said. 'Arrange for a replacement' said I. "That's your problem John, the company won't replace that, the only thing they will replace is the beer python but every other working part in the building is down to you." It seemed that I had just been shit on from a great height, to cut a long story short it cost me 2'500 pounds for a new generator.

A few weeks later I was having a late drink with my bar staff and a few friends when Sue one of my bar staff pointed to the back bar and said, " I think you have a leak John." I turned around casually expecting to see a drip of water, not a fucking waterfall cascading down the full length of my back bar. 'Bloody hell where the fucks that coming from? I shouted. I know it was pissing with rain outside but now it was as wet inside as it was out. I quickly got the ladder and shot up it to have a look in the loft, it was pissing in through a long section of wall, D.I.Y Dave had joined me. "It s coming from the walk way to the flats, the drains must be blocked; the water has no where to go so its found a weak point and coming through the lower wall." We must have both had the same thought at the same time, we both made a dash for the ladder, we were down the ladder and out the side door and up the stairs to the flats inside two minutes and he was right, the walk way was like a lake, I imagine some of the flats already had water in their hall ways. BROOMS! Dave and I said in unison as we turned and legged it down the stairs. We returned with two very large brooms and side by side we commenced to sweep the water down the stairs, we were soaked and laughing at the same time, as we sang Old Man River.

The following morning I was straight over to the council building, which was directly opposite the Pride. Within half an hour I had somebody out inspecting the damage because I said, where the water had come through it ran over a lot of wiring which is a fire hazard if it shorts out. Within two days they cleaned the drains and re-damp proofed the walls. We were getting nice little crowds in so I decided to start up a lottery draw within a week we had around forty people signed up, then I introduced them to Take Your Pick. At the time I was the only pub or club in Milton Keynes playing the game, we started of with six envelopes, three held money prizes and three held booby prizes, depending on how many raffle tickets I sold would determine how much money would be put in the envelopes, the booby prizes would consist of a packet of crisps, a bag of pork scratchings, or a pound to play next weeks take your pick. If the envelope with the most money in (known as the jackpot) was not won, it would rollover to the following week. By law I was only allowed to go as far as 999 pounds 99 pence, to go that extra penny I would have to apply for a gaming licence, but having said that, we had it up to a £1000 on a number of occasions. Once the jackpot had reached £500 I had to get extra staff on Sunday mornings because my pub was full of people from other pubs that wanted to try their luck, of course I knew which envelope the jackpot was in and if somebody picked the right envelope, I would do my best to try and tempt them to take the money I was offering them for their envelope, nine times out of ten they would take the money, say for instance the jackpot stood at £260 I would count out into their hands seventy pounds very slowly then stop abruptly and say, that's it no more money, they have got seventy pounds in their hands, then I would say, it could be a booby your holding, (a packet of crisps,) or it might even be the jackpot, but if it is a booby, your going to be right sick turning down seventy pounds, its practically guaranteed that they will keep the seventy quid, then when I open the envelope and show them the piece of paper with jackpot written on it, they not only look sick they feel sick, so not to make them feel so bad, I would ask them how many raffle tickets they brought, if they had only brought one strip which had cost them a pound, I would say, smile, your sixty nine pounds better of than when you started and you never walked away with a packet of pork scratchings, that normally cheers them up a bit. It took about three months before the other pubs in the area caught on, then my Sunday trade went back to normal, but we did gain a few Sunday soft drink customers.

The thing I was mostly known for in the Pride was the kids fun days, the O.A.Ps parties, and for putting Bingo on twice a week (Wednesdays & Sundays).

Now, could you imagine in your wildest dreams me as a bingo caller, no wayeeeeee.

Yes, from a he-man butch wrestler to a bloody bingo caller. I don't know whether they really came for the bingo or to see me calling out silly numbers to dodgy rhyming slang, well, which ever it was we were getting the pub full on those two nights. It all started one Wednesday night, there were only about fifteen people in the bar and I was bored, so I went in the office and brought out a little kids bingo toy. I went round to all my customers and told them to give me a pound. What for? They asked. 'Just give me a pound and you will find out' I said. So each and every one of them gave me a pound. 'Right' I said, 'now we are going to play bingo.' I'm not playing bingo one or two of them said. 'I have your pound which your not getting back and the winner of the game gets the lot.' So I dished out the cards and we started to play. Looking back its quite funny to see some of the Lakes Estate hard men sitting there playing bingo, and after one of them won, asking for another game, as I said, it was only a kids toy with beads as numbers, I had to turn this handle to get the beads out and if I turned it to fast the bead would fly out on to the floor. There were a couple of old boys that wanted to play and they seemed to enjoy themselves. The following week they were back and asked if we were going to play bingo again, they had brought a couple of friends from Bramley Grange the O.A.P place just up the road. I explained to them that it wasn't a proper game of bingo, more a laugh, and depending on how many played what the prize money would be, in all we had about twenty players, and we played around five games, and a couple of times the old people won. Later that evening one of them asked me to make up a bingo poster and he would put it up in the Grange advertising the bingo at the Pride. I said I would do that and give it to him next week, The following week he was back with at least seven of his friends from the Grange, there was also a few more of my regulars coming out on a Wednesday to play bingo and I was still using the kids bingo toy, it only stood about eight inches tall and six inches wide. I've now got all these people coming in to play bingo, can you imagine what they were thinking when they saw this big black geezer sitting there with a toy bingo board in front of him, and a little bubble with beads in with a tiny little handle on the side, ready to call house on bingo, I can, their thinking this is got to be a fucking joke,

So like a good pro I turned it into a joke, every number I called there was a funny or saucy rhyme to go with it, like, 'knock at the door out comes a whore' number four, or the one they liked best 'John's favourite,' and they would all shout out 69. It didn't take long before I had to fork out for a proper bingo board and start giving away some decent prize money, we still played the game with tongue in cheek, but when it came to the jackpot round we played the game properly, and if it was not won in a certain amount of calls it would be rolled over to the following week. My dead Wednesdays had now turned into bonanza midweek of over a hundred people, as it was going so well I decided to try it on a Sunday night, and again I had hit the jackpot.

But all good things come to an end, there were two things that happened in quick succession that brought a closure to the bingo, one was an idiot who came in and gave a lot of abuse to his misses, so I asked him to leave, and he didn't want to, so I took him by the arm and he pulled away, he was having none of it, I asked him to leave again, he started to walk towards me and as he did I noticed he was clenching his hand into a fist, I waited until he wrong footed himself then hit him with a right hander that would have dropped Mike Tyson, but all he did was stagger back a few steps and said, "is that the best you've got?" I hit him with a left and a right that knocked both the studs out of his eyebrows and still he stood there, so I hit him full force straight in the sternum, he folded over so I took him by his dyed bleached blond hair which I had wrapped around my hand, I was either going to pull his hair out, or his head off, but as I gave an almighty great yank, some of his hair was wrapped around one of my fingers and it pulled it to one side, and in doing so broke it. I'm afraid I really lost it at that point, I dragged him outside and used his face as a punch ball and I only stopped when I couldn't hold my arms up any more, I then went back inside and apologized to all my customers. Later that night someone set fire to my cellar doors. I don't know whether I was meant to believe it was the big mouth idiot who did it, but I just knew it wasn't him because that wasn't his M.O, he would put a pool cue across the back of my head when I wasn't looking or hit me with a shovel from behind, but to set fire to my doors, no that wasn't him.

Saturday lunchtime I had not long been open when I noticed shit head walking past my windows heading towards the pub door, I got there before him to stop him coming in. 'What do you want?' I asked. "I've just come to tell you I had nothing to do with that fire the other night." 'I know that, I didn't think for one moment you did.' He went on to say, "I don't know what you fucking hit me with the other night but I keep getting bloody head aches, I'm off to see the doctor." 'Only my fists' I said, 'and if you wasn't so stoned out of your brain box you would have dropped with the first punch and you wouldn't be looking like John Merrick the elephant man.

A week or two later It came to light who had set fire to my cellar doors, and he also got a slap.

I had a falling out with one of the girls who came to the bingo, and to show how vindictive she could be, she stood over by the shops nearly all day Monday and everyone she saw that came to the bingo nights she told them that I had stopped doing the bingo. When Wednesday came around I only had about thirty faces in. 'Quiet tonight' I said. We heard you had stopped doing the bingo but we had to see for ourselves. 'Who said I had stopped doing the bingo?' I enquired. No one could point a finger as they all had heard it from someone else. 'Well if the jackpot goes tonight its their loss" I said. I never expected to see any of the old folk in because of what had happened the previous week, if I were them it would have scared the shit out of me as well, some of the old dear's were visibly shaking when they left that night, I couldn't apologise enough, they didn't need to see that shit on their night out.

One name kept cropping up when I was asking around for the person who said the bingo had finished, and it turned out to be the person I fell out with.

So I had enough. I did stop the bingo but I stopped it in my favour, the jackpot stood at six hundred and twenty five pounds, half went to a charity and the other half went to me. I say it went to me but indirectly it went to the Grange. I put it towards the Christmas party we were arranging. Every year except for the first year, we gave the Pensioners of the Lakes Estate a Christmas party, paid for mostly by the patrons of the London Pride, the Pride may have had a bad reputation, but the customers weren't shy in putting their hands in their pockets when it came to charities.

They did the same when I suggested a fun day for the kids. We started raising money from January doing all sorts of things It was community spirit at its best, we had charity head shaves, hairy guys being waxed, baby in the pram competitions, so called hard men dressed as babies being pushed around in a pram collecting money, what silly bastard is going to take the piss out of them, and if they said put, "something in the bucket," you can bet your sisters virginity that they put something in. I had a chart on the back bar that showed every week what had been collected. We always had the fun-day on the third or forth Saturday in the kids summer holidays. Some times we made it theme day and some of the girls in the pub would dress up. We hired a bouncy castle, face painters and clowns. A friend of mine always lent us his disco so we had music. I set up the Bar-B-Q and got a volunteer to cook, and of course there were the stocks, and muggings here were always the first to go in. All the kids could eat and drink for nothing, but the adults had to pay for their hot dogs and burgers, be it only fifty pence but you would be surprised how many sent their kids up to get one for nothing, the tight bastards. A week before the kids were due back to school we always took a coach load down to the coast for the day, not me I'm not that stupid, but I had eight mums that volunteered, each had about six kids to look after, we did this with the money that was left over from the fun-day, one time there was enough left over for me to stand at the coach door and give every child that got on a fiver spending money which worked out to be around £220. A few days after they got back one of the parents came in for a drink and said, "you know, I gave my two kids twenty Pound each to spend on that day trip you arranged, and all they kept saying when we picked them up was Johnny Kincaid gave us a five pound note each," I laughed and said, 'I have to look after my future punters.'

After twenty one years in the trade I started to feel the pinch, it had already cost me my relationship with Jean, the trade was dropping off at a fast rate, and

I couldn't think of anyway of pulling it back, there is only so much you can do to or for a pub on the Lakes Estate and I had done the lot. Sainsburys had started to sell discounted cans of beers and spirits to keep up with Tesco's, then a new shop opened called Bargain Booze selling even cheaper cans, was it worth keeping my off Licence open, was it hell, so I sold of my existing stock and closed my off sales. About four month prior to this the Brewery thought it was the right time to up my rent, I argued the point to no avail, so I tried to sell my lease on. By the time I came out of The London Pride I had

been there nine and a half years. For a year and a half the pub was on the market and in that time I didn't have one straight buyer. 'I have had enough' I said, and I eventually walked away, not completing my ten-year lease and losing my entire fixture and fitting money.

Now to finish on a good note. After twenty three years of never having a Christmas or New Year off, it is so nice to be able to relax, have a drink with my friends and family and not having to worry about the atmosphere or the tension in the air, not having to worry about getting pissed and closing the pub, don't get me wrong, I enjoyed my time doing a job I loved, and I met my new partner Hazel whilst doing it, but there comes a time when you have to call it a day, so I decided to call time, for the last time on June the 2nd 2005.

ABOUT THE AUTHOR

This is Johnny's second book on his Biography, the first one depicted his early life being born and brought up in Battersea, (not Barbados) how he got in trouble and was put in a home, and how after doing a spell in a Detention Centre he ended up on a travelling fair ground, he joined a boxing and wrestling booth taking on all comers. Johnny was only into boxing in those days, but one of the wrestlers (John Monk) started to train Johnny and from there on he never looked back. His wrestling took him all over the world to some weird and wonderful places. He has met a King, a Prince, and many famous people through his travels, there were also many women around who wanted to keep company with our Johnny, and Johnny always said that he was put on this earth to spread happiness, so he spread as much as possible.

This book is more about the later part of his career, when leaving the fame and glory behind and becoming a publican, how his life changed in many ways and in other ways it never did. How pub punters picked on him because of what he used to do for a living. Johnny said it was some times like being back in the ring; the only difference was that he wasn't being paid for it. He tells some stories that will make your hair curl, about what some pub punters do when they think their not being watched.

Johnny said that he has had two major jobs in his life; he wrestled for twenty-six years then went in to the pub game for another twenty-three years, and one way or another they were just the same.

Like everybody, Johnny has had his ups and downs, his highs and lows, but the in betweens have been very exciting, and this is what he wants to share with you, so take a walk in Johnny's shoes and meet the Hawaiian dancer who did the hip job on him, and how he met the Rock for the first time. Take a ride through seven of his pubs and see if you can pick out anyone you might know, but be warned, although there are no names mentioned, you might just recognise yourself.